Hidden Treasures

CORNWALL

Edited by Allison Dowse

First published in Great Britain in 2002 by
YOUNG WRITERS
Remus House,
Coltsfoot Drive,
Peterborough, PE2 9JX
Telephone (01733) 890066

All Rights Reserved

Copyright Contributors 2002

HB ISBN 0 75433 900 9
SB ISBN 0 75433 901 7

FOREWORD

This year, the Young Writers' Hidden Treasures competition proudly presents a showcase of the best poetic talent from over 72,000 up-and-coming writers nationwide.

Young Writers was established in 1991 and we are still successful, even in today's technologically-led world, in promoting and encouraging the reading and writing of poetry.

The thought, effort, imagination and hard work put into each poem impressed us all, and once again, the task of selecting poems was a difficult one, but nevertheless, an enjoyable experience.

We hope you are as pleased as we are with the final selection and that you and your family continue to be entertained with *Hidden Treasures Cornwall* for many years to come.

CONTENTS

	Shannon Parkes	1
Alverton CP School		
	Adam Freethy	1
	Scot Davies	2
	Emma Lainchbury	2
	Lucy Payne	2
	Heleena McCrindle	3
	Michael Hicks	3
	Zoe Robinson	3
	Sophia Cowburn	4
	Robert Noall	4
	Perran Andrews	5
	Kelvin James	5
	James Mark Sampson	6
	Charlotte Matthews	6
	Michael Eddy	7
	Laura Smith	7
	Rebecca Goody	8
	Kelly Jewell	8
	James Roberts	8
	Lee Webb	9
	Katy Talbot	9
	Ben Nowell	10
	Ryan Holland	10
	Robert Allen	11
	Laura Matthews	12
Biscovey Junior School		
	Jack Clark	12
	Daniel Hart	13
	Jessica Thompson	13
	Rebecca Clarke	14
	Kirsty Burt	14
	Ayesha Curtis	15
	Jordan Truscott	15

Sara Dorrington	16
Sherrilynne Hearn	16
Brandon Tregidgo	17
Ashley Mason-Maxwell	17
Chelsey Johns	18
Vanessa Collings	18
Alisha Biggs	19
Lauren Bowker	20
David John Tregonning	20
Nicole Prynn	21
Catherine Gill	22
James Horton	22
Rochelle Kidd	23
Rebecca Pereira	24
Joanne Allen	24
Josh Truscott	25
Shezad Ali	26
Thomas Cox	26
Claire Case	27
Gary Camps	28

Camelford CP School

Lucy Gillmon	28
Sam Smith	29
Josh Smith	29
Lauren Wickett	30
Joseph Driscoll	30
Alexander Macleod	31
Abigail King	31
Adam Piper	31
Jessica Brookham	32
Daniel Piper	32
George Hollidge	32
Sadie Cornelius	33
Josh Barron	33
Courtenay Parsons	34
Bryony Ferrett	34
Martin Heal	35

	Reece Williams	35
	Lisa Pedlar	36
	Lisa-Marie Sneddon	36
	Betty Alexander	37
	Jessica Ellison	37
	Samantha Claydon	37
	Melissa Luffarelli	38
Cury CE Primary School		
	Lisa Johnson	38
	Jade Watkinson	38
	Hannah Kenworthy	39
	Rachel Bennett	39
	Corey Fletcher	40
	Charlotte Bradbury	40
	Victoria Hale	40
	Katrina Mills	41
	Rachel Minchin	41
	Kieren Watkinson	42
Cusgarne CP School		
	Katie Johns	42
	Sarah Kersley	43
	Lucy Ackerman	43
	Merryn Thomas	44
	James Rimmer	44
	Lewis Hobbs	45
	Freya Van Hoorn	45
	Tom Duddle	46
	Harvey Collins	46
	Jessica Long	47
	Georgina Sherriff	47
	Mollie Davidson	47
	Alyssa Pay	48
	Jeni Woolcock	48
	Richard Gorman	48
	Martin Sherriff	49
	Reba Laity	49

Chris Ockwell	49
Jenna Gazzard	50
Daniel Crewes	50

Ladock CE Primary School

Helen Sincock	51
Marya Hicks	51
Katie Hoskings	52
Catherine Eslick	52
Aaron Bawden	52
Douglas Moore	53
Christopher Gregory	53
Jessica Milling	53
Robin Nicolle	54

Mithian Primary School

Esmé Kerton	54
Morgan Dallyn	55
Shannon Russell	55
Wilf Waters	56
Ciaran Barry	56
Mhairi Purves	57
Sally Carlin	58
Abigail Rowland	58
Hannah Parry	59
Anna Hunt	59
Emily Coyle	60
Daisy Kemp	60

Mount Charles CP School

Katy Notley	61
Elwyn Moreton	61
Jazmine Lovatt	62
Channelle Venning	62
Sammy Thomas	63
Eleanor O'Shea	63
Josh Ridgment	64
Kieran Miller	64

	Sarah Matthews	65
	Daniel Eden	66
	Naomi Solomon	66
	Esther Rich	67
	Luke Stevens	67
	Jemma Lobb	68
	Mary Pantling	69
	Zoe Matthews	70
Mullion CP School		
	Guy Olliff	70
	Lee Marchant	71
	Laura Woolford	71
	William Sherlock	72
	Thomas Bray	72
	Robyn Rowarth	73
	Mathew Geach	73
	Patricia Lepper	74
	Andrew Greet	74
	Thomas Rendall	75
	Yasmin Cottrell	75
	Daniel Wilson	76
	Cai Dale	76
	Sophie Enever	76
	Joe Page	77
	David Cattran	77
	Lee Cattran	78
	Jon Lewis	78
	Ruth Oliver	79
	Sarah Harding-Wilson	79
	Nathan Davison	80
Nancledra CP School		
	Harry Williams	80
	Emily Becalick	81
	Ella Frears Hogg	81
	Alice Freeman	82
	Chris Lanyon	82

Nanpean CP School

	Charlie Goodchild	83
	Tamsyn Fulbrook	83
	Laura Hampton	84
	Aaron Fowler	84
	Samantha Marshall	85
	Joanne Knowles	86
	Kirsty Burford	86
	Jade Stephens	87
	Katy Philp	87
	Sean Hambly	88
	Joseph Hawes	88

Penponds School

	Zackary Such	89
	Samuel Jones	90
	Hanna-Marie Creese	91
	Emma Bingham	92
	Michael Cowley	92
	Melodie Jade Such	93
	Christopher Quigley	93
	Elizabeth Nidds	94
	Shay McCauley-Dawes	94
	Gemma McCormick	95
	Elinor Weedon	96
	Bethan Pugh	96
	Lauren Battershill	97
	Emma Rowe	98
	Charlotte Wandless	98
	Rosanna Roberts	99
	Joe Weeks	100
	Thomas Heywood	100
	Kelly Symons	101
	Abi Skewes	102
	Tamsyn Allen	103

Perranporth CP School
- Gavin Parker — 104
- Ted Allsop — 104
- Adrian Hennuyer — 105
- Ryan Barnes — 105
- Ellie-Jae Lewis — 105
- Abigail Brandreth — 106
- Amy Voyce — 106
- Lucy Rickett — 107
- Karina Davis — 107
- Jannah-Beth Lucas — 108
- Joshua Hider — 108
- Georgina Musselwhite — 109
- Joseph Miller — 109
- Emily Horrigan — 110

Polruan CP School
- Jessica May Palmer — 110
- Joseph Tomlin — 111
- Mathew Beresford — 111
- Tom Nutland — 112
- Rhys Lamy — 112
- Jasmine Libby — 113
- Emma Nutty — 114

St Breaca CE Primary School, Helston
- Daniel Warden — 114
- Ben Powell — 115
- Juliet Robertson — 115
- Michael Worden — 116
- Georgia Harrison & Charlotte Wells — 116
- Georgina Wells — 116
- Rosie Woodman — 117
- Rosie Reynolds & Chloe — 117
- Jessica Harrison — 117
- Ben Watters & Perry Ware — 118
- Ailsa Sutherland — 118
- Merryn Tresidder & Michael Hall — 119

Felix Lovell & Sam Ratcliffe	119
Gemma Reid	120

St Columb Major CP School

Marcus Lukacs	120
Carly Rundle	121
Jenna Rundle	121
Millie Norris	122
Jodi Aldridge	122
Rachel Batchelor	123
Nicole Braden	124
Charlotte Sztajneet	124
Korrie Hegarty	125
Aimee Passmore	125
Natalie Pearce	126
Joanna Powell	126
Caitlin Baker	126
Louise Culley	127
Rosina Pappin	127
Christine Billingham	127
Joe Slack	128
Annie Brown	128
Danielle Wadd	129
Leigh Brooks	129
Jade Barrasin	130
Shannon Smith	130
Laura Barrasin	131
Danielle Platt	131
Sarah Chapman	132

St Mary's RC Primary School, Falmouth

Lewis Johnson	132
Joseph Halloran	133
Rebecca Telling	133
Emily Jorey	134
Daniel Turner	134
Daisy Roberts	135
Thomas Edgerton	136

Jake Scrace	136
Senara Chesher	137
Coral Andrewartha	137
Marty Conlon	138
Cody Cooke	138
Sally Morrison	139
Samuel Richardson-May	140
Rebecca Parsons	140
Jake Pellow	141
Paul Bacchus	141
Katie Dunford	142
Elliot Webb	142
Daniel Rudall	143

St Tudy CE Primary School, Bodmin

Poppy Yeomans	143
Jack Yeo	144
Adam Matulewicz	144
Christopher Simmons	144
Brian Stidwell	145
Jessica Mann	145
Emma Northcott	146

St Wenn Primary School, Bodmin

Heidi Thomas	146
Sophie Thomas	147
Michael Clarke	147
Min Kybett	148

Sandy Hill Primary School

Leepa Begum	148
Sam Woolhouse	149
Kelly Maby	149
Hannah Goodwin	150
Kimberley Johns	150
Matthew Pope	151
Kimberley Mills	151
Charmaine Vague	152

Kate David	152
Philippa Anderson	153
Kaylee Harrison	153
James Palmer	154
Laura Shepperd	154
Matt Trethewey	155
Paul Gill	155
Barney Mathews	156
Ryan Boxall	156

Shortlanesend Primary School

Emily Hinkley	157
Brandon Light	157
Suzanne Reeves	158
Rachel Parry	158
Hayley Robins	159
Holly Wenna-Hegarty	160
Annette Hodges	160
Adam Wells	160
Gareth Reeves	161
Aimee Wonnacott	161

Tregony CP School

Rosalind Lytham	162
Rowan Heather	162
Verity McIntosh	163
Daniel Grayston	163
Daisy-Elizabeth Jones	164

Upton Cross Primary School

Daniel Campbell-Harris	164
Emily-Rose Clay	165
Millie Parrott	165
Danielle Elizabeth Mayors	166
Joshua Turner	166
Kathy Dilworth	167
Gemma Stephens	168
Carys Barriball	168

Lucia Szweda	169
Terry Northey	169
Victoria Anne Moyse	170
Mark Weeks	170
Georgina Lucas	171
Elizabeth Joy Cowan	172
Holly Beale	172
Catherine Cole	173
Katy Bartlett	173
Louise Grace Barriball	174
Emma Bunney	174
Alice Colligan	175
Adam Carthew	175
Bethany Louise Plummer	176

The Poems

WHEN I WAS...

When I was one I looked at the sun,
The sun was too bright, it gave me a fright.
When I was two I looked at my shoe,
My shoe was black, I thought it was my cat.
When I was three I climbed a tree.
When I was four I saw a door.
When I was five I took my first dive.
When I was six I chopped some sticks.
When I was seven I thought I was eleven.
When I was eight I had my first date.
When I was nine I learnt to rhyme.
Now I am ten let's do it again.

Shannon Parkes (10)

SHIPWRECKED

A ship is wrecked near the land
The sea is rough and moves the sand
The wreck is buried under the sand
Its treasure no more to be found
We dived and dived and looked at the ground
Under the sea around and around
Something shimmers in the sand
And we bring a box to the land
We open it up and what do we find?
Treasure and jewellery and things of that kind
We take it home to look at forever
Because it is our secret treasure.

Adam Freethy (11)
Alverton CP School

CHILDREN'S TREASURES

When I go to the beach
I like collecting shells, stones and driftwood
And smell the smells of the open, wide sea
It's good to look in rock pools, you find some special creatures
You see them in the sea, you see them in the rock pools
They swim, they glide,
It's just as fast as you going down the slide.

Scot Davies (10)
Alverton CP School

CHILDREN'S TREASURES

Children's treasures are cuddly and soft,
too good to put in the loft.
Children's treasures aren't silver and gold,
they are bright and bold.
Children's treasures aren't windy and dull,
children's treasures are bright and beautiful!

Emma Lainchbury (9)
Alverton CP School

CHILDREN'S TREASURES

CDs and tapes they're all fun
I don't mind a currant bun
I like playing with my teddies
I also like to save my pennies
I like colouring and drawing
And it's never boring.

Lucy Payne (10)
Alverton CP School

MY TREASURE

H is for my hamster that is my treasure
A is for active because she is
M is for munching because that's what she likes to do
S is for Sweetie because that is her name
T is for true because she's a true part of me
E is for enjoyable because she fills me with glee
R is for rose because I think she is one
    That's my treasure!

Heleena McCrindle (10)
Alverton CP School

MY TREASURE TROVE

My mum is my treasure
Because she is cuddly and sweet
Just like a teddy bear she is warm and soft
I love her lots because she's my mum
She's my treasure trove.

Michael Hicks (10)
Alverton CP School

CHILDREN'S TREASURE

Different children have different treasures
Some are large, some are small
But each and every one brings great pleasure
Toys and animals are two of many
But one child's treasure might be a penny
One child's treasure might even be the whistling of the waves
from the big blue sea.

Zoe Robinson (10)
Alverton CP School

A Child's Treasure

A treasure can be many things
A toy, a photograph, a lock of hair
But the most treasured of all is a memory
You can hold it in your head and keep it there.

It can be a smell, a taste, a soft touch
A picture in your mind
A time when you were happiest
Or when someone special was very kind.

Sophia Cowburn (9)
Alverton CP School

My Hidden Treasure

I have a hidden treasure
It's red
It's a love-giving pump.

I have a hidden treasure
It's small
It keeps me alive.

I have a hidden treasure
It's my life.

I have a hidden treasure
It's my heart.

Robert Noall (10)
Alverton CP School

CHILDREN'S TREASURES

I'd rather have a dog
Than a frog
My dog's called Kelly
She has a small belly.

When we're walking
I do the talking
She wants to play
Every single day.

She comes when I call
Cos I've got her ball
If I didn't have a dog
I'd have to have a frog.

Perran Andrews (9)
Alverton CP School

WHERE IS THE TREASURE?

Take ten steps out of the sea,
Then to your left should be a tree.
Take some steps to the right,
Until you are in line with the light.
Walk forward five steps,
Push the bolder into the sea.
Look over the rocks and you will see,
You have opened a door,
To reveal the treasure once more.

Kelvin James (11)
Alverton CP School

HIDDEN TREASURES

H idden treasures under the sand will it ever be found?
I stand where the X covers the treasure
D anger for the pirates speeding through the rapids
D own the waterfall shaking like a leaf
E dging closer to the hidden treasure
N oise of the pirates' shovels scraping up the sand.

T he treasure will give the pirates lots of pleasure
R ushing pirates zooming to get the treasure
E choes at the bottom of the pirates' pit
A nxious pirates longing for the treasure
S hips rushing to the treasure island
U nder the sand lies the hidden treasure
R uins of other ships that crashed on the rocks
E nd of the pirates' journey for gold
S ailing back with all the gold.

James Mark Sampson (11)
Alverton CP School

CHILDREN'S TREASURES

When I was three
I loved my trike
Now I am older
I've a suspension bike
My friends were mad
When it became boys, boys, boys
We played with our make-up
But boys play with smelly toys.

Charlotte Matthews (10)
Alverton CP School

Hidden Treasure

We have often strolled past that door
The green one at the top of the steps
We have often wondered what was behind it
A witch, some monsters there had been kept?
One day we were brave and decided to look
Just like the stories in the book.

We crept up the stairs one at a time
Hoping that everything would be fine
We tried the handle but it would not move
The paint on the door was not very smooth.

We tried it again and this time it turned
My goodness, inside we squirmed
Would it be witches or monsters? We did not know
In a minute we'd have to go!

A beautiful view greeted us as we opened the door
A hidden garden of flowers covered the floor
Daffodils, bluebells, foxgloves galore!
The hidden treasure behind the green door!

Michael Eddy (10)
Alverton CP School

Children's Treasure

My treasure is gold
My treasure is very old
My treasure is funny
My treasure is yummy
My treasure is sunny
My treasure is runny.

Laura Smith (10)
Alverton CP School

TREASURES

My dad is a treasure because he's always there
Sometimes he looks at me with a stare
My dad is a treasure because he teaches me lessons I have to know
He takes me places I want to go
My dad is a treasure because he loves me lots
When doing the dishes he dries the pots.

Rebecca Goody (10)
Alverton CP School

TIME

Time passes
Day after day
Leaving happiness and sadness
Along its way
Not knowing
What the time will bring
A newborn child
Or maybe a king.

Kelly Jewell (11)
Alverton CP School

CHILDREN'S TREASURES

A treasure is a pleasure, a very wonderful toy
It might be for a girl, it might be for a boy
Big treasure, small treasure, old treasure or new
It doesn't matter to me or to you
Look after your treasures, treat with care
Then when you are older they might still be there.

James Roberts (9)
Alverton CP School

IN THE DEEP

In our trusty boat
Jon, Fred and me
Set off to do some fishing
On the deep blue sea.

Fred put on his diving suit
And dived into the deep
Excited he rose up again
With a great big leap.

He found a galleon on her side
That sank many years ago
So down we went to have a look
For treasure far below.

Underneath some wreckage
Some coins we did find
Silver plates and silver spoons
On the deck did lie.

We made our way back to land
Excited with our lot
Treasures that years ago were buried and forgot
And laid there far below.

Lee Webb (10)
Alverton CP School

THE JEWELS HAIKU

The gnarled hands grabbed it
The treasure chest creaked open
The jewels glinted.

Katy Talbot (11)
Alverton CP School

HIDDEN TREASURE

My bedroom is a treasure chest
Mum said she is going to tidy my room
Oh no! I dread to think what she may find!
The wrappers of last year's Easter eggs
My missing socks
But . . . on the other hand . . .
She may find long forgotten treasures . . .
The screws for my skateboard
The stash of Christmas money I've been secretly saving
The missing piece to complete my jigsaw
The last lost block for my Lego model
The needle for my football pump
The cheats for my computer game
My long-lost library book
But most of all I hope my mum will find my homework
Because it is due in tomorrow!

Ben Nowell (11)
Alverton CP School

BEDROOM TREASURE

My bedroom is full of toys
Hidden treasure to my baby brother
Locked away so he can't play
Things to make and break
I hide the key so he won't see
I know he longs so much to touch
If only he could find the key
I know that he would want to be
Playing with my hidden treasure
My bedroom is full of toys.

Ryan Holland (11)
Alverton CP School

HIDDEN TREASURE

There is treasure in the cloakroom
Treasure in my bed
Treasure under the sofa
Treasure in my head
Treasure is the best
This is my treasure chest

There is treasure on the island
Treasure growing on trees
Treasure on the pirate ships
Treasure under the seven seas
Treasure in the hold
Treasure on the deck

Treasure hidden in my pirate's boots
Treasure in my favourite place
Treasure in my pockets
Treasure in every space
Treasure is made to share
Treasure can be found everywhere

We will always need treasure every day
And so that means it will never die.

Robert Allen (11)
Alverton CP School

HIDDEN TREASURE, WHERE COULD IT BE?

Where is that treasure, for we have to find it to take over the world
It could be under our feet right now
Or it could be over there under the sand that remains still and silent
It could be under that rock over there
Which is as hard as a dinosaur's bone
It could even be on that boat over there
Which rocks like it's in a stormy winter's night
Or was the treasure just in their imagination?
We will never know.

Laura Matthews (10)
Alverton CP School

HIDDEN TREASURE

H idden treasure
I t's down there
D ead eels
D ead people
E els guard treasure
N asty night.

T errifying swords
R aggy flag
E vil bone
A ll the things
S keletons looking at you
U nder the sea
R usty penny
E nding with memories.

Jack Clark (9)
Biscovey Junior School

HIDDEN TREASURE

H ats and scarves lie on the seabed
I n the sea there's no sound
D eep down
D ark down at the bottom of the sea
E els guarding a treasure
N ice, expensive on the bottom of the sea

T reasures guarded
R are gifts
E xpensive treasure
A ring has rusted
S ilently lying there
U nderneath the depths
R ubies gleaming
E verything's calm.

Daniel Hart (8)
Biscovey Junior School

OLD AGE AND YOUTH

Old age is green and slimy
It smells like burning hot baked beans
Old age tastes like slimy rats' tails
It sounds like a scream of a girl
It feels soft and sharp
Old age lives in a dark cave in the middle of a lake.

Youth is yellow and brown
It smells like a bunch of flowers
Youth tastes like a warm bread
It sounds like an egg boiling in a pan
It feels like a big ball
Youth lives in a cupboard.

Jessica Thompson (9)
Biscovey Junior School

HIDDEN TREASURE

H idden down there
I n the
D eepest
D arkest
E ver ocean
N o one's ever been there

T reasure down there
R usting and broken
E els guarding their nephews
A ll dark and
S ilent
U nder the ocean
R usting as can be
E els are swimming free.

Rebecca Clarke (8)
Biscovey Junior School

LIFE AND DEATH

Death is hot and red
It smells like burning steam
Death tastes like dreadful cuts
It sounds like a bombed rocket
It feels like slithering gunge
Death lives in a dark, creepy cave.

Life is shivering blue
It smells like chopped up apples
Life tastes like hot jam
It sounds like switching lights
It feels hard and lumpy
Life lives in a world.

Kirsty Burt (10)
Biscovey Junior School

KEY

I open doors that are magic
And lead into adventures
Fun and magic places
I am not any ordinary thing
And I am the only one that is alive
I am gold and round
I am lots of shapes
I am long and short and hard
I am really fun inside
I open thoughts and dreams
I can take you into mermaid land
Where knights and dragons
Horrible beasts and monsters live
I can take you into fantasy land
I can take you into scary stuff
And unlock doors that have magic gardens
I hold the future for wherever you want to go.

Ayesha Curtis (9)
Biscovey Junior School

OLD AGE

Old age is purple and gritty
It smells like burning lava
And tastes like grass or mud
And it sounds angry and horrible
It feels slimy and slippery
And it lives in a mouldy cake.

Jordan Truscott (9)
Biscovey Junior School

HOPE AND DESPAIR

Hope

Hope is pink, so bright
A lovely smelling rose
Hope tastes like sugar
It sounds like a humming bee
Ticklish and funny
It lives in the heart of a sparkling diamond.

Despair

Despair is navy blue and dark
It smells like burnt toast
It tastes like ginger beer
Sounds like a scream of horror
Feels like grimy bones
It lives in the heart of a black widow.

Sara Dorrington (9)
Biscovey Junior School

A LEAF

A leaf can be green, brown, yellow or red
A leaf can be beautiful with a flower
A leaf is part of nature
You can't pick a leaf or it will die
Leaves belong to trees
Some leaves like cabbage are food
Leaves are the shape of teardrops.

A leaf is my hidden treasure
Because a leaf should live and die when it's ready.

Sherrilynne Hearn (8)
Biscovey Junior School

HIDDEN TREASURE

H idden treasures under the sea
I n an old ragged ship
D ead fish
D ead people
E verything quiet
N othing moves

T reasures guarded by giant fish
R ed rubies
E els guarding too
A ll this time people trying to get the treasure
S ecret chambers lead to the ship
R usted gold
E nd of the wreck.

Brandon Tregidgo (9)
Biscovey Junior School

WAR AND PEACE

War is black
It smells like petrol drifting over men
It tastes sick and cold
War sounds like shells falling from the sky
It feels cold and pointy
War lives in the centre of a bomb.

Peace is blue
It smells like sweets in a shop
Peace tastes like melted chocolate
It sounds like children in a playground
Peace feels smooth and warm
It lives in the heart of a human.

Ashley Mason-Maxwell (10)
Biscovey Junior School

HIDDEN TREASURE

H idden in the seaweed
I t's near to the shipwreck
D eep down
D own deep under the waves
E veryone listening to the news
N ever a trace of treasure

T iptoeing divers swim around
R otten bones afloat
E els glide across the sea
A xes and swords on the floor
S and is covering all the ground
U gly octopi start to wake
R ubies glistening
E veryone looked but nothing was found.

Chelsey Johns (9)
Biscovey Junior School

FEAR AND BRAVERY

Fear

Fear is purple
It smells like burning trees in the forest
Fear tastes like grit and is stony
It sounds like whirring wind whirling around
It feels like hailstones hitting your hand
Fear lives in the crevice of the Earth.

Bravery

Bravery is blue
It smells like good luck coming your way
It tastes like cold Lucozade fizzing in your mouth
Bravery sounds like loads of people cheering for you
It feels like you're a champion
Bravery lives deep, deep in your heart.

Vanessa Collings (10)
Biscovey Junior School

HIDDEN TREASURE

H ave you seen
I n the dark sea
D eep
D eep in the sea
E els guarding
N o one has seen it

T ry to spot it
R emember it
E veryone will know
A ll alone
S lowly walk
U nder sea
R emember
E very tale.

Alisha Biggs (8)
Biscovey Junior School

HIDDEN TREASURE

H idden treasure that no one knows
I n the sea where no one goes
D ivers have not been found
D eep, deep down
E els guarding the wreck
N o one knows what's down there

T he fishes swimming around
R are sharks chasing around
E nter the world of the ocean
A nchors lost deep in the sea
S ee the jellyfish wriggling
U nder the sea where fishes are attacking the waves
R eturning to the sea
E nding the fun in the sea.

Lauren Bowker (9)
Biscovey Junior School

MY MAGIC TV

My magic TV
It has a golden rim
Plus a silver grin
It's round like a football
I'm proud of my TV!

My special TV
He's cool like me
It's better than me
So hee, hee, hee
My TV is simply the best!

My big TV
He's beautiful like me
Nothing's better than my TV
He smells like rubber
I feel good about my TV!

My bumping TV
Can be as loud as a rugby match
My TV can turn into a DVD!

So my TV is way better than your TV!

David John Tregonning (9)
Biscovey Junior School

HIDDEN TREASURE

H idden treasures
I dentity not been found
D eep down
D own in the ocean
E els going mad
N ever been found.

T reasures gleaming
R eels being wound up
E xpensive gifts
A nybody can see it
S harks guarding treasure
U nderneath the muck
R ubies shining
E verything calm.

Nicole Prynn (9)
Biscovey Junior School

HIDDEN TREASURE

H ave you heard?
I n the ship
D own underneath the sea
D iamond jewels
E meralds sparkling as bright as can be
N obody has seen the jewels because

T errifying animals guard the ship
R ainbowfish swim on by
E agles look down
A ncient treasures may be there
S harks hiding waiting to swim out
U se special gear, you may be safe
R ocks have battered the ship
E nding memories will be left.

Catherine Gill (8)
Biscovey Junior School

DEATH AND BIRTH

Death

Death is dark and black
It smells like mouldy rags in a bin
Death tastes crisp and sour
It sounds like a raging volcano
It feels like a blade of steel
Death lives in a cold, damp swamp.

Birth

Birth is bright and silver
It smells like a sweet flower
Birth tastes like a lovely strawberry
It sounds like a beautiful flute
It feels soft like pure silk
Birth lives in your heart.

James Horton (10)
Biscovey Junior School

HIDDEN TREASURE

H ave you seen?
I am telling you
D iving under the deep blue sea
D ragons diving guarding
E els stalking around
N o one knows about it.

T reasure is shimmering like
R ed rubies
E ating eels
A ll the monsters guarding around
S melly food everywhere
U nusual fish swimming around your head
R eally scary but hidden treasure
E verybody dead but it is a secret.

Rochelle Kidd (9)
Biscovey Junior School

HIDDEN TREASURE

H ave you seen
I n the
D eep dark
D eep ocean
E nding with tales
N umbers had death.

T reasure hidden
R emember the story
E els guarding
A ll dark and
S till
U nder the world
R emember
E nding with memories.

Rebecca Pereira (9)
Biscovey Junior School

DEATH AND BIRTH

Death

Death is black and brown
It smells like flesh that's been in your attic for a year
The taste is like really gone-off bread
And sounds like screams of horror
The feel is sore and spiky
It lives in the deepest part of a cellar.

Birth

Birth is the lightest gold
It smells fresh and new
And tastes like a meal fit for a king
Birth sounds like sweet, sweet music
It feels like a new beginning
And lives in your heart.

Joanne Allen (9)
Biscovey Junior School

HIDDEN TREASURES

H idden in the depths
I t's very quiet and dark
D arkness everywhere
D aylight nowhere to be seen
E verywhere silent
N ot a sound to be heard.

T ales of pirates and
R ed rubies
E els guarding the treasure
A nybody's treasure
S alty seas
U ndergrowth
R eels wound in
E verybody knows.

Josh Truscott (8)
Biscovey Junior School

HIDDEN TREASURE

H idden skulls under the sea
I t's never been discovered
D ead people
D aggers and swords
E els guard their homes
N othing there can be.

T reasures guarded
R otting clothes
E ggs rotting of the pirates' food
A nts from the surface
S nakes
U nder the sea
R otting people
E nding of memories.

Shezad Ali (8)
Biscovey Junior School

WAR AND PEACE

War

War is black
It smells like smoke burning
It tastes warm and wretched
War sounds like shrieking men
It feels rough and spiky
War lives in the centre of a piece of coal.

Peace

Peace is yellow
It smells like buns baking
Peace tastes warm and sweet
It sounds like children singing
Peace feels soft and squishy
It lives in a big heart.

Thomas Cox (10)
Biscovey Junior School

HIDDEN TREASURE

H ave you seen the treasure
I n under the sea
D eep down
D ark as can be
E els swim free
N o one's ever been there before.

T reasure is lying down there
R usty as can be
E els guarding the gold
A ll dark and grey
S ilent shivered
U nder the sea
R usty as can be
E verlasting memory.

Claire Case (9)
Biscovey Junior School

DEATH

Death is a very terrible colour
It smells like hot blood
Death tastes like people's smelly breath
It sounds like eerie voices
It feels like boiling sweat
Death lives in a fiery cave.

Gary Camps (9)
Biscovey Junior School

WHAT I THINK

Flowers are beautiful and romantic as love
Dancing under the gods above
Hearing fireworks go boom, boom, boom
Makes me run and hide in my room
Out in the garden in the dark
Lovely displays begin to spark
All the sky is full of stars
And far beyond are Venus and Mars
I see the moon so bright
Shining through my window at night
Sometimes the clouds hide its face
Making it look like it is in disgrace
I love to see a shooting star
It is the most beautiful by far
I make a wish, hope it comes true
If it doesn't, never mind I won't get blue
There is a rainbow for all to see
Making wonderful colours in the sky for me
The world we live in isn't so bad
But sometimes things that happen make me sad.

Lucy Gillmon (9)
Camelford CP School

THE LAKE MONSTER

Down in the creepy forest lies a Loch Ness monster
Some say it's not true
But you hear a slithering through the water
Children get scared when they see his slimy dark hair
His tail grows like a fast motorcar
Once it has stopped growing it's like a 20 foot lake
Some say he's green, some say he's purple
But nobody cares because they're scared when he gurgles
No one knows what he exactly looks like
It doesn't matter, they just don't want to
Because if they do they will *scream* for help
And then the scary old grandpa would cut off its long tail
And eat it for his dinner.

Sam Smith (9)
Camelford CP School

MONSTROUS POEM

The bell goes, there's an empty school
The kids run out
Some are playing in swimming pools and they shout
When it's empty monsters come out
And no one knows that they scream and shout.

At night they party all night
People planning robberies and they call them traitors
At light they get a fright all right
And now they're haters
But at night they frighten people all right
And they put walls up to stop traitors.

Josh Smith (9)
Camelford CP School

The Garden

The garden is empty,
No children inside,
The garden is empty,
Just like the sky.

Leaves fall from the trees,
And the garden is empty,
There's a gentle breeze,
The garden is empty.

No flowers are there,
The garden is empty,
It is so bare,
And the garden, empty.

The smell is so earthy,
But still the garden is empty.

Lauren Wickett (10)
Camelford CP School

The Nintendo

N othing better than a good game to play
I nside and out of the rain
N othing can disturb you if your brother's tame
T ons of screaming and shouting
E very day you hear
N othing now because you are here
D emonstrate you can play for hours
O n the Nintendo instead of picking flowers.

Joseph Driscoll (9)
Camelford CP School

MY FRIEND JOE DRISCOLL

My friend Joe Driscoll from France
Once forgot to put on his pants
He went to Big Ben
At half-past ten
Then he was infested by ants.

Alexander Macleod (9)
Camelford CP School

THE SHINING STAR

The shining star
Gliding through the sky
Glittering, gleaming
Wonderful dreaming
All on a winter's
Night.

Abigail King (10)
Camelford CP School

THE DIRTY HABIT POEM

There was an old missus called Jenny
Who had a fat husband called Lenny
And he picked his nose
Sucked his toes
And had a best friend called Benny.

Adam Piper (9)
Camelford CP School

THE SHEEP

There once was a sheep called Doodle
He had a friend that was a poodle
The sheep was small
And the poodle was tall
And their favourite meal was noodles.

Jessica Brookham (10)
Camelford CP School

THE CAVE

T here are lots of spooky monsters
H iding in spooky dark places
E ating all the cave

C an we be brave?
A ll slimy and damp
V icious creatures underneath the ground
E xploring the cave!

Daniel Piper (9)
Camelford CP School

POETRY

P unctuation
O n poetry has a good affect
E very sentence has a full stop
T ry to use it all the time
R eveal your true power of poetry
Y ou could be a star.

George Hollidge (9)
Camelford CP School

THE EMPTY CLASSROOM

The school desks creaked
The windows smashed
The blackboard squeaked
The doors went crash.

Outside the thunder is rumbling
Inside the mice are squeaking
Outside the ghosts are mumbling
Inside the classroom is reeking.

You can hear the clock - tick-tock, tick-tock
You can hear the bell - ding-dong, ding-dong
You can hear the tap - drip-drop, drip-drop
You can hear the drums - bang, bang, bang, bang.

This classroom is deserted all the children say.

Sadie Cornelius (9)
Camelford CP School

THE CAVES

T here are lots of spooky monsters
H iding in the darkness
E ating all the food they can find.

C atching lots of spiders
A t the strike of midnight
V acuuming them all up
E njoying watching them in the cupboard
S aving them for Easter Day to eat with roast duck.

Josh Barron (9)
Camelford CP School

THE EMPTY CLASSROOM

The classroom is now empty
The windows creak with relief
Shh! Shh! Shh!
The chairs sit comfortably
The lights hum in harmony
The curtains dance in the dusk
And it is very peaceful.

The classroom is now full
The chalk screeches against the board
Chatter! Chatter! Chatter!
The children laugh and talk and moan
The bell jingles, the feet tingle
To get to the door
Once again it is peaceful.

Courtenay Parsons (10)
Camelford CP School

THE YOUNG GIRLS

There was a young girl in year six
Who liked collecting sticks
She picked up a log
And looked at a frog
Oh, what a terrible fix.

There was a young girl in year five
Who wanted to get to St Ives
Her mum said no
But she wanted to go
Because everyone there has nine lives.

Bryony Ferrett (9)
Camelford CP School

MY FRIENDS

My friend Alex Macleod from Spain
Once was in a lot of pain
He fell down the stairs
For one of his dares
Then became insane.

My friend Adam Piper from Pakistan
Once decided to move to Afghanistan
He lived in a hut
With a smelly old mutt
Then decided to move to Milan.

My friend Josh Baker from New York
Once decided not to eat pork
He didn't like the city
I thought that was a pity
Because he always bent his fork.

Martin Heal (9)
Camelford CP School

MONSTER

M onster in a closet
O n the run from me
N asty and very naughty
S tealing all he sees
T ramping everywhere
E ating all our food
R un the sun is up
    Goodbye!

Reece Williams (10)
Camelford CP School

WHAT IS FIRE?

A roaring dragon
Breathing fire
And hot burning flames

                        A golden flame
                        Burning all colours
                        In the sun

A blazing fire
Warming people
On a cold winter's night

                        A spark of lightning
                        Bolts across the sky
                        Fire springs to buildings

A candle burning
In the darkest forest
At night.

Lisa Pedlar (9)
Camelford CP School

A NEW SPRING DAY

As the sun sets, spiders' webs glimmer in the cold moonlight
Spring is here
Baby animals are being born
Buds are growing into beautiful flowers

In the morning the new spring flowers open
A new spring day is here
All the new babies are now a day old
And are walking on their four legs.

Lisa-Marie Sneddon (9)
Camelford CP School

PARENTS

P laying football in the house, no way!
A t the park after school, think again!
R acing in the garden, why don't you do something quieter?
E ating between meals, never!
N othing to do and nowhere to go
'T is boring in his house
S o go away and play!

Betty Alexander (10)
Camelford CP School

THE SWIRL

The swirl is blue and white swirling to and fro
I like to watch it swirling in the moonlight sea
With the white sea horses dancing.

Jessica Ellison (9)
Camelford CP School

ANIMALS

A lligators are fierce carnivores
N ight's when the lions come out
I n the afternoon galloping zebras
M ice crawling through holes
A ntelope rushing through the waters
L eopards sleeping in the sun
S uch things live in the jungle.

Samantha Claydon (10)
Camelford CP School

THE SEA POEM

She lives in the sea, not like me
She is blue, not like you
She is like glitter, not all bitter
She is nice, not like mice
She is lovely and bubbly
She's a little baby dolphin.

Melissa Luffarelli (10)
Camelford CP School

MY GUINEA PIGS

Guinea pigs are very sweet
Standing on their tiny feet
Munching apples, grapes and carrots too
These are the things they like to do
But they also like to make friends with you.

Lisa Johnson (9)
Cury CE Primary School

MY MUM

My mum is great, she isn't fake
She keeps her word, she's the best thing in the world
She has four horses, they keep us busy
We have two dogs, they are very silly
She is on a diet because she is plump
She's got to work hard at it to get rid of the bump!

Jade Watkinson (10)
Cury CE Primary School

POP IDOL

There once were a hundred
Now there are two
Which one will win?
It's all up to you
They'll sing their songs
And the judges comment and joke
Then we'll wait for the result
After we've made our vote
Is it Gareth with his stammer
Or Will smiling at you?
I know who I'd vote for
Can you guess who?

Hannah Kenworthy (11)
Cury CE Primary School

SPLISH, SPLOSH, SPLASH

Splish, splosh, splash
Dancing in the rain
Jumping in the puddles
Running down the lane.

Splish, splosh, splash
It's coming down again
I have to stay inside
Which is such a shame.

Rachel Bennett (9)
Cury CE Primary School

RED ANTS

Three red ants running and playing
Having a quarrel
One red ant had the flu
When they had a leg count
There were only two

Two red ants running and playing
Having a quarrel
One red ant went to see Don
When they had a leg count
There was only one.

Corey Fletcher (8)
Cury CE Primary School

TYLER AND FLORRY

My cat Florry,
Give it ten years she'll be as big as a lorry.
Her coat is as black as night
With a tint of light.
But my cats really fight.
Now my cat Tyler, he's a bit of a live wire
And his coat is like a pattern of a tyre.
They're both strange cats,
But they are good at getting *rats!*

Charlotte Bradbury (9)
Cury CE Primary School

TALI

Tali is my pony
He's not thin or bony
He's got a bright white face
So you can see him even when you're in space.

He's accompanied by friends
Whose love for him never ends
He never gets lonely
For he is my pony.

Victoria Hale (10)
Cury CE Primary School

WINNIE THE POOH

Winnie the Pooh is my favourite bear
He eats honey all day
He has lots of friends that are made of fur
Why not love him, you don't have to pay.

There's Tigger, Piglet, Kanga and Roo
And lots more friends to play
So don't you worry, he's very friendly
You can love him all of the day.

Katrina Mills (10)
Cury CE Primary School

SPRING MEADOW

I sit in a wild spring meadow
With sweet smelling flowers in my hand
What is beyond the rusty old gate?
Where is the rest of the land?

I'm all alone while I sit
In the meadow that is now cold as ice
No one is around me
Only the tiny brown mice.

Rachel Minchin (11)
Cury CE Primary School

TIGERS

Two bouncing tigers
Jumping through a tree
Twisting and turning
Catching a bee
One bouncing tiger
Went to find John
When they had a tooth count
There was only one!

One bouncing tiger
Jumping through a tree
Twisting and turning
Catching a bee
One bouncing tiger
Went into the jungle deep
You could not count his teeth
When they had a tooth count
Because he was asleep!

Kieren Watkinson (7)
Cury CE Primary School

WHEN I WAS YOUNG
(Inspired by Charles Causley)

When I was young
I lived in Lanner
I used to mend things
With my spanner
I knew a man
Who rode a bike
I asked his name
And he said Mike.

Katie Johns (8)
Cusgarne CP School

THE NEWSAGENTS
(Inspired by Margaret Blount)

'Would you like some sweets with some Turkish treats?'
'No, just some popcorn please.'
'Or would you like some Quavers in three different flavours?'
'No, just some popcorn please.'
'Would you like some jellybeans or maybe some salad cream?'
'No, just some popcorn please.'
'Would you like a chocolate biccy? They are very nice and sticky.'
'No, just some popcorn please.'
'Would you like a Daily Mail or a birthday card that wails?'
'No, just some popcorn please.'
'Would you like a tasty pasty? I promise you they don't taste nasty.'
'For goodness sake, I want some popcorn please!'
'OK, OK, calm down, but tell me one thing, why didn't you say so?'

Sarah Kersley (10)
Cusgarne CP School

SPRING'S COMING

The dew swept grass sways under the cool breeze of the morning
As the golden sun sets over the shimmering sea
It turns crisp golden, red and yellow
The sun dances high in the sky watching, waiting for the newborn
They're coming
The bright, smiling daffodils shine like suns
Swaying in the wind in time, dancing to the song of spring
Trees blossom, bushes bloom, look around you and *wow!*
It's beautiful.

Lucy Ackerman (10)
Cusgarne CP School

THE PET SHOP
(Inspired by Margaret Blount)

'Would you like an African cat, or perhaps a vampire bat?'
'No, just a dog please.'
'Or some trapezing fleas, they drink cups full of tea?'
'No, just a dog please.'
'We've got tropical fish, they make quite a dish?'
'No, just a dog please.'
'A rare find we have is an Antarctic lizard, she was found in
                                        such a terrible blizzard.'
'No, just a dog please.'
'A pure white unicorn with a mystical horn?'
'For goodness sake, *I want a dog please!*'
'OK, but why didn't you say so?'

Merryn Thomas (10)
Cusgarne CP School

AT THE DUMP

The old, punctured tyres being tossed around
like tarnished copper coins.
The thousands of lorries clamber over the anthill of rubbish
engines roaring like dragons.
The seagulls swirling, whirling, hurling high
now descending on their luxurious feast.
The abandoned, creaky cookers sit there stiffly
with the rust scraping at their sides.
The air's natural ways are disturbed by the thick throat-choking
fumes from the roaring monster-like rubbish lorries.

James Rimmer (11)
Cusgarne CP School

THE TREASURE CHEST
(Inspired by Kit Wright)

I will put in my treasure chest,
The spine-chilling cold of a frosty winter's day,
The soft fall of a raindrop from a black-grey sky,
The low moaning of sailors lost long ago just off the Cornish coast,
The ear-splitting sound of nails on a blackboard,
The scuttle of a terrified mouse,
The first gurgle of a happy baby.

My box is forged from silver, gold and steel
From the far corners of the Earth.
With a cobra for a handle, a deadly snake's sting for a lock
And a snake's tongue for a key.
It's embroidered with hair from a woolly mammoth.

Lewis Hobbs (9)
Cusgarne CP School

THE TREASURE CHEST
(Inspired by Kit Wright)

I will put in the treasure chest
The last light of a silver glittering moon
And the swish of a dog's golden tail
A silver lake of ice-cold snow
One minute from an old long forgotten clock
A smooth silver dolphin somersaulting into the silent sea
A white soft swan diving into ice light water
The first miaows of a newborn tabby cat
A loud roar from a frightening tiger.

Freya Van Hoorn (9)
Cusgarne CP School

THE TREASURE CHEST
(Inspired by Kit Wright)

I will put in my treasure chest
The first soft miaow of a newborn kitten
The final glitter of a glinting moon
The long-lost howl of a wolf, in the tall mountains
The drop of a leaf on an autumn day
The loud bang of a hammer on a huge nail
The lovely smell of a golden brown Cornish pasty
The excitement of children on their birthday
The speed of an ostrich as it bounds across land
The swish of a sparkling fish's tail as it darts through the deep
The loud neigh of a horse through grassy plains
The swirling of grey mist on a dark night on Bodmin Moor
A drop of rain from a horrible, misty, grim day
The sweet dreams of children as they drift off to sleep
The huge loud roar of a lost and lonely lion
My box is forged from gold, silver and jewels
From an ancient secret cave
With the hoot of an owl on the lid and a tusk for the handle.

Tom Duddle (9)
Cusgarne CP School

ANGER

A ripping tornado thrashing against buildings
spinning rapidly like a giant's whirlpool
smashing anything in its way.
A terrorising streak of lightning
bursting through rough, dark clouds.

Harvey Collins (9)
Cusgarne CP School

Despair

Stuck in a traffic jam, cars as far as the eye can see, never ending.
Waiting silently in a jammed lift with somewhere important to go.
Walking and walking in a gloomy tunnel, legs getting tired
trying to find the end.

Jessica Long (8)
Cusgarne CP School

Cat

The cat is beautiful, sleek and shiny
Purring by the Rayburn
Licking her paws.

A scruffy alleyway cat
Hissing at dogs as they pass the dustbins
Barking.

Georgina Sherriff (9)
Cusgarne CP School

Innocence

A small white crab scuttling lightly
across the clear golden beach.
A clear morning sky with the sun blazing
giving heat ray to light the world.
A golden field full of ripe corn
swaying gently in the breeze.

Mollie Davidson (9)
Cusgarne CP School

SUMMER

Lying on the warm, gold sand in the scorching sun building sandcastles
Swimming in the crystal clear sea, leaping and jumping like dolphins
The smell of sausages sizzling on the barbecue
People come around to have parties on the patio in the evening sun
Orange, red, yellow smudging together to make a perfect sunset
like a patchwork quilt covering the Earth
Lying in a tent in a warm sleeping bag in the middle of the woods
camping out, telling each other scary stories on a clear summer's night.

Alyssa Pay (10)
Cusgarne CP School

STORM

The lightning angrily split the star-littered sky
The thunder rolled loudly down a hill
The wind blew strongly, rattling all of the trees in its path
The rain heavily hammered the rooftops of houses
The storm raged on through the night until it got tired
And dozed off into a deep sleep.

Jeni Woolcock (10)
Cusgarne CP School

STORMY SEA

The ferocious sea slashes itself against the slippery rocks
Waves the size of a cliff
The current as strong as a horse
The dangerous sea as rough as a stone.

Richard Gorman (10)
Cusgarne CP School

THE DUMP

Heaps of bags on top of bags filled with nothing but rubbish.
Rubbish pouring all over, lorries continuously coming from nowhere.
An old bike with one wheel is propped against a washing machine
                                    that nobody wants.
The JCB shovels the rubbish around and around into a gigantic heap,
getting bigger and bigger.

Martin Sherriff (11)
Cusgarne CP School

RIVER

R ivers are sometimes so fast that
I wouldn't want to go swimming
V ery fast rivers rushing rapidly sometimes flooding
E verywhere, every day
R ushing, every minute rising *everywhere!*

Reba Laity (9)
Cusgarne CP School

THE FURY OF THE SEA

Boats are tossed and thrown around
Shores brutally beaten and battered
Lightning tears and shreds at the sky
Waves challenge the lighthouse by lashing out at it with rage
Surf is scattered across the sea while in the distance the light
from the village glows snugly.

Chris Ockwell (11)
Cusgarne CP School

EARLY MORNING

Cold, heavy and frosty dew lay lightly on the gently swaying grass
the greenness of the grass has faded overnight,
The quiet sensation is wrecked by the noises that are made
like pins being forced into cushions,
The red, yellow and orange sun rises slowly through the sky
leaving the hill behind lonely and lifeless,
The sound of young wildlife energetically running into the peaceful
outside world,
People quietly and restlessly eat their delicious breakfast
and discuss the magnificent morning and how tranquil it is,
Children, as they enter school, smile like a Cheshire cat
but moan in despair as they cannot be outside playing.

Jenna Gazzard (10)
Cusgarne CP School

EVENINGS

As the evening invades the afternoon
The red-hot blazing sun is running down the sky like a golden lion
The smell of smoke is reaching the street, hovering
Trying to get in every gap as slowly as a snail
The street lights try to break through the mist to light up the sky.

As the evening invades the afternoon
The foxes are creeping out of nowhere like an ant
Taking its chance to hunt
The evening forms a ginormous blanket of silence over the street
Then gradually turns to black.

Daniel Crewes (11)
Cusgarne CP School

MY DAD

My dad is a man that uses some sand
To build when he can and he works by hand
He rests sometimes with a glass of wine
When building a kitchen made of pine
After making a dent, he mixes cement
When using a pole, he fell in a hole
My dad is good when sawing some wood
When he's building with stone he uses his mobile phone
Then he rings to tell us he's on his way home
When he gets home he does nothing but moan
But I really do love my dad.

Helen Sincock (9)
Ladock CE Primary School

THE BIRD'S NEST

I saw a bird's nest
One of the very best
There was a bird in
And some newborn chicks
They made an awful din.

Then the bird stared at me
Flew up and down like a bumblebee
Took a glimpse, then zoomed to the food table
Brought back a beak full of food
Then fed some to the chicks, unable.

Marya Hicks (9)
Ladock CE Primary School

BUTTERFLY

Coloured wings,
Gently flap against the wind,
Small, black body,
Another story,
Fighting to stay alive.

Katie Hoskings (10)
Ladock CE Primary School

THE LITTLE HEDGEHOG

I looked out of my window
And saw a spiky thing
Funny nose, electric head
What a funny thing.

I put out bread and milk
He scoffed it all up
And licked his lips and smiled
Oh, what a funny thing!

Catherine Eslick (9)
Ladock CE Primary School

SUMMER DAYS

The birds are swooping in the sky
The lakes and ponds are getting dry
The boys are playing water fights
The girls are launching off their kites
The summer days are heating up!

Aaron Bawden (11)
Ladock CE Primary School

SHARK

Hidden in the deep blue sea
Hidden in a dark blue cave
Eyes of white
Teeth are red
A shark just ate human flesh.

Douglas Moore (10)
Ladock CE Primary School

BEACH

B each, beach you are so great
E very day we come
A nd play on your sand
C liffs crumbling down onto you
H orses ride on your sand.

Christopher Gregory (11)
Ladock CE Primary School

SPRING CINQUAIN

Watching . . .
As the sun gleams,
Gleams upon the meadow,
See the lambs as they skip and play,
See them.

Jessica Milling (10)
Ladock CE Primary School

MR FRONE

The only time I'm all alone
Is without my teddy, Mr Frone
When we named him
Mum said, 'Fred'
And Dad said, 'Bone'
So I've got my ted
Mr Frone.

I like to think my teddy's real
I make him eat at every meal
Teds are great
They're fluffy, they're small
No battery changes at all!
But *my* teddy's special
He goes with me to bed
Then, at about half-past eight
'Time for bed,' he said.

Robin Nicolle (9)
Ladock CE Primary School

MIDNIGHT

Midnight, midnight
With your stars so bright
Midnight, midnight
Shine the moonlight
Midnight, midnight
The time that bats take flight
Midnight, midnight
Help me sleep tonight.

Esmé Kerton (8)
Mithian Primary School

THE MAN-EATING SNAIL

Captincan, Captincan met a man-eating snail
Captincan, Captincan on the night he got his mail.
The snail was big, the snail was slimy
He ate people down and made them grimy.
The snail saw Captincan
And remembered he liked to eat man.
He ate his liver raw
And then he ate some more.
The navy came all the same
They shot the snail down
And all at once he fell right to the ground.

Morgan Dallyn (10)
Mithian Primary School

LOWENNA, LOWENNA

Lowenna met a giant called Catherine
Lowenna, Lowenna asked to come in a Lowenna, Lowenna
                                                          asked to come in.
The giant was happy, the giant was glad
The giant was messy, big and bad.
The giant said, 'Lowenna, how nice to see you
Now it's time to try and eat you.'
Lowenna, Lowenna, didn't care
Lowenna gave her a boot in the air.
She did her hair and climbed up the stair
And at the top she ate a pear.

Shannon Russell (9)
Mithian Primary School

SPRING

Winter is fading into the night
the frosts are melting,
the earth is warming,
the sun brings life.

Dawn brings the chorus
of nesting birds
with hope and joy
of new life in spring!

Flowers burst forth
from their deep sleep
nudging the soil
up, up, up, up.

Bluebells are ringing
bringing spring to the woods
as the rain pitter-patters
gently down, down.

As animals stretch
from their long winter's sleep,
we all feel the difference
of spring in our reach.

Wilf Waters (8)
Mithian Primary School

RIVER LIFE

By the river, animals hop and hide
In the river fish swish and glide
Frogs hop here and there
Insects crawl everywhere.

Dragonflies dance in the shimmering light
While freshwater crayfish fight
Sapphire colours, a kingfisher in flight
Oh, what a beautiful sight.

Ciaran Barry (8)
Mithian Primary School

TEACHER'S PET

The teachers in my school must think they're working in a zoo.
Their classrooms feature many a creature, but here are just a few;
Mrs Read has a centipede, it jumps about and wriggles,
But when it's time, it gives us all the giggles.
Mr Parkinson has a ten foot bison, it really makes a commotion,
But when it's time for show and tell, we say we found a python.
Mrs March has a six foot larch, she said she bought it in today,
But now it's home time, we all get to go away.
Mrs Young found mighty Joe Young upon a hill with trees,
We brought it back, it hurt its back,
So we had to mend its knees.

Linda has a reindeer in her backpack for lunch,
Now he's getting too heavy, we had to throw him in a bunch.
Miss Gilman has a Doberman,
Don't give me the idea that it's going to eat us,
Let's all run out of here.
But young Miss Treat, so nice and sweet, has the best pet there can be,
I hope she'll never change that pet
For young Miss Treat has me!

Mhairi Purves (9)
Mithian Primary School

UP IN THE SKY

U p above the land all day
P egasus and friends will play.

I n the sky there are some kites
N obody there ever fights.

T he clouds may rush by
H umming a lullaby
E verybody looks up as one

S kipping along is such fun
K eeping together as we fly
Y es, it's good to go so high!

Sally Carlin (9)
Mithian Primary School

UNICORN

Unicorn playing in the sky,
Watching comets flying by.
As one neighs to another,
As one plays with her brother
And one runs to its mother.

Little unicorn flying in the sky
As their daddy creeps by
And the little one tries to fly.

Abigail Rowland (8)
Mithian Primary School

TIGERS

The tiger sits and lies in wait,
I would not go a-walking,
It may be your fate.
Going through the jungle,
The shadows and the light,
Even in the day you may get scared,
But at night you may get a bigger fright.
Ravenous tigers stealthily slip
This is an animal you may not want to miss.
Shy, beautiful tigers hide all day,
They are a creature you should obey.

Hannah Parry (10)
Mithian Primary School

PONIES

As the ponies gallop over the sand,
The mane flies just like a bird,
The sand leaps up into the air,
The ponies gallop faster and faster,
Then you see the splashing of the waves.

Ponies frisk about in the field,
As you see them gallop about,
Their long manes flying in the air,
The green grass changes to mud
As they gallop past,
What fun to be a pony.

Anna Hunt (10)
Mithian Primary School

THE MERMAID

The mermaid sits on her rock all day
Combing her golden hair
She flicks up her tail and jumps up high
And does a somersault in the air.

She sits on a rock
In a turquoise lagoon
She wakes up at night
And sings to the moon.

She plays with the dolphins down in the sea
She thinks it's fun
Splishing and sploshing
And smiling with glee.

She plays with the seaweed
Puts shells in her hair
Sings to the fishermen
Till her hair goes fair.

Emily Coyle (9)
Mithian Primary School

AUTUMN FROST

The frost snaps, the flowers flee,
Followed by the bumblebee.
Birds fly back to their nests,
So they can have a peaceful rest.
Cotton wool-tailed rabbits scurry,
Off to their burrows they must hurry.
Summer has gone for another year,
It is time for winter to reappear.

Daisy Kemp (8)
Mithian Primary School

THE FAMILY'S SECRET

Once upon a stormy night,
the moon lit the sky with a bright, white light.
The gloomy house stood on the hill
and as we arrived we felt a chill.

As we opened the door it creaked,
we crept into the hall and heard a screech.
We climbed the stairs, our hearts were thumping,
we were so scared our nerves were jumping.

Along the corridor we saw a light,
an elegant lady dressed in white.
She sang a sad and meaningful song,
a song of warning and terrible wrong.

We fled from the house and never returned,
and since that day, strange things we've learned.
The family that lived there mysteriously died,
except one . . . I survived!

Katy Notley (9)
Mount Charles CP School

THE PLANETS

Jupiter, Saturn, Uranus and Neptune have rings,
They are giants, wonderful things.
On Earth you can have lots of fun,
Venus and Mercury burn like the sun.
Mars is red, a rocky ball,
Pluto is coldest and smallest of all.

Elwyn Moreton (9)
Mount Charles CP School

MY RECORDER

I was determined to learn my recorder,
but I didn't listen to my teacher.
I thought it would be easy,
but it became harder.
I tried to persevere,
squeak, whistle, squeak,
So then I did listen to my teacher speak
and it became clearer.
Oh good, oh glee,
I was getting nearer.
My parents recognized the tune I played,
now I was learning,
I was playing, 'London's Burning'.

Jazmine Lovatt (9)
Mount Charles CP School

PETS

I like big pets
I like small pets
I like dogs
I like cats
I like pets
My horse is a pet horse
I like horses
I like rats
and I like mice
I like
Pets!

Channelle Venning (9)
Mount Charles CP School

ALL ABOUT DOLPHINS

My favourite things are dolphins,
They move like the wind
Dancing amongst the trees.
They swim like fish,
Shine like the sun
And jump up and down with fun.

They call and shout
Until you come,
They sing and dance and hum.
The dolphins dance like ballerinas,
Over the waves
They glide and gaze.

They move as flexible as eels
Darting in between the water plants,
Playing with trout,
Cods searching for their meals.

Sammy Thomas (11)
Mount Charles CP School

COLOURS

Blue is like the breeze on a sunny day,
Pink is like a picnic in the park,
Yellow is like chatting inside on a rainy day,
Red is like a just-picked, sparkly rose,
Purple is like going to a party with your mates,
Black is like an end of a poem, dull and boring.

Eleanor O'Shea (9)
Mount Charles CP School

THE DOOR

Open the door
You will find
A sheep with pink wool
Or a pig with red skin
Or a cow that is yellow
Open the door
You will find
An owl that flies at night
Or a cat that sleeps on the mat
Open the door
You will find
A fire-breathing dragon
Or a scaly fish
Or a smelly sock
Open the door
And you will
    Be in
        Paradise!

Josh Ridgment (11)
Mount Charles CP School

TODAY IS VERY BORING

Today is very boring,
It's a very boring day.
My hair is like a hedgehog
And a mouse is in my tray.

I'm stuck in my classroom
With a boy called Wayne,
He's fat, he's tall,
He picks his nose
And he's a terrible pain.

It's raining cats and dogs,
I don't know what to do,
There's a giant kissing the piano
And my teacher's got the flu.

Kieran Miller (10)
Mount Charles CP School

THE TIGER'S LIFE

The sun was a beaming ball of fire
Above the greenest trees,
Down below the treetops high,
There was a buzzing hive of bees.
The stony path was sunlit,
'Twas leading to the lake
And the tiger came running,
    running, running,
And the tiger came running for his belly's sake.

After the lake he could see his food,
If he couldn't get over he would get in a mood.
He looked up, he could see the trees
Blocking the sun above the big, black cloud.
Buzzing around the food was the hive of bees,
He tried blowing them away with a cool breeze.
He shouted, 'Go away.' He said it really loud.

He had to swim across the lake,
Otherwise his poor belly would break.
He had to get there just in time,
The tiger went racing, racing, racing.
The tiger came racing, to eat his meat and live.

Sarah Matthews (10)
Mount Charles CP School

My Magic Box

In my magic box I would put the heart of a lion, so strong and beastly.
In my magic box I would put the feel of flying with the wind
                                                               in my face.
In my magic box I would have the knowledge of an owl.
In my magic box I would put the whistling of the wind.
In my magic box I would put the softness of a cloud, so fluffy
                                                                 and white.
In my magic box I would put the life of a flower, so happy and good.
In my magic box I would put the laugh of a hyena.
In my magic box I would put the speed of a cheetah.
In my magic box I would put the roar of a tiger.
In my magic box I would put the reflection shining on the
                                                               flowing water.
In my magic box I would put the winning goal with the keeper
                                                             diving but missing.
In my magic box I would put the sea smashing against the rocks.

Daniel Eden (11)
Mount Charles CP School

Dreams

D oorways and gates reveal imaginary fates,
R ooms full of flowers standing for hours,
E ver rising staircases taking me to different places,
A lways travelling away to return for the new day,
M ysterious noises come from the wall, it sounds like a whale call.
S ounds have gone, I must go before the morning show.

Naomi Solomon (9)
Mount Charles CP School

LOVELY CORNWALL

Pasty, post, beaches with golden sand,
Paddling in the sea, teddy in my hand,
All the fishermen coming back from sea,
Oh, there's a miner, 'Come and talk to me.'
Sheepdog here and there, they're all around,
Digging their wet noses in the ground.
White and black cross in the middle,
I fall in the soggy sea, 'Oh fiddle.'
Gooey, sticky, yucky clay,
Nut-brown horses eating golden hay.
Going to the 'Eden Project', yeah,
They grow lots of coconuts covered in hair.
Now my holiday comes to its end,
I thank lovely Cornwall for being my friend.

Esther Rich (10)
Mount Charles CP School

TODAY IS VERY BORING

Today is very boring,
I'm hardly having fun,
Godzilla's on the loose again
And my brother's got a gun.
It's the beginning of the Apocalypse,
What a boring day,
It's raining poison acid,
I want to go and play.
Today is very boring,
There is an escaped rhino,
There is a rat on the lino,
There are people threatening the school,
Today is so uncool.

Luke Stevens (10)
Mount Charles CP School

My Dog

My dog is the best in the world,
The universe, the sky.
If you listen carefully, I'll tell you why.

He's as brave as a lion,
As courageous as a bear,
He's as cunning as a fox
And he's as clever as a hare.

He's as quick as a cheetah,
As sneaky as a cat,
He's as sly as a snake
And as tricky as a rat.

He's as cheeky as a chimpanzee,
As lively as a hog,
He's as sleek as a leopard
And as jumpy as a frog.

He's as cute as a koala,
As chatty as a goose,
He's as playful as a puppy
And as proud as a mouse.

He's as fantastic as a peacock,
As wonderful as a quail,
He's as cool as a polar bear
And as bold as a whale.

He's as creepy as a spider,
As dotty as a hen,
He's as slick as an eel
And as witty as a wren.

Some people say he's the most
Daring dog of all time,
But in my eyes he's perfect,
Because he's all *mine!*

Jemma Lobb (8)
Mount Charles CP School

You!

You!
Your hair is like the gold sunshine.
You!
Your eyes are like blue jewels.
You!
Your nose is wet like a dog's.
You!
Your lips are like roses.
You!
Your ears are like little raindrops.
You!
Your cheeks are soft like a baby's bottom.
You!
Your shoulders are big and muscular.
You!
Your belly is like a strongman's.
You!
You're big and round like a big balloon.

Mary Pantling (10)
Mount Charles CP School

COLOURS ARE LIKE...

Blue is like the bouncy beat of a song,
So catchy you want to sing along.
Pink is like a pretty princess
In a tower with a pretty pink dress.
Green is like a grassy bank by a river,
But don't fall in or else you'll shiver.
Purple is like the planet party,
Everybody's laugh is hearty.
Orange is like a flickering fiery flame,
Don't get too close, play the game.
Yellow is like a yummy melon,
Not as sour as a lemon.
Red is like a royal rose,
A valentine kiss I suppose.
Black is very boring,
Just like the end.

Zoe Matthews (9)
Mount Charles CP School

THE FINALOGY

The finalogy I'm about to show you
has unfortunately got the flu.
There is a tumultuous tribe
that I can only begin to describe.
Their eyes are an unusual red,
their bellies bulging with thread.
There are steel spikes on their backs
that are deadly and deeply black.
A mind as full as Einstein's
and the strength of Frankenstein.

Guy Olliff (11)
Mullion CP School

THE HOUSE ON THE MOOR

Under rotten floorboards there might have laid bodies,
If you entered you would find out with ease
Because people say along the old coast,
There is an old house swarming with ghosts.

Only the swaying swampland trees
Can see the gruesome dead zombies,
But you can still hear the groans
Of the lifeless skeletons' bones.

It may send a quiver down your spine,
But don't stop to shiver at the sign.
Stay away from the house on the moor!

Lee Marchant (10)
Mullion CP School

UNICORNS

Unicorns dwell in people's minds and in their imaginations.
They're magic and beautiful creatures,
Manes as fine as the finest lace,
Fur that reflects the moonlight
As they walk down to the water to drink.
Their golden hooves sparkle in the sun
And they have a horn like twisted toffee.
The most desired thing on Earth.
Just because you don't see them,
Does not mean they don't exist.

Laura Woolford (10)
Mullion CP School

A LIE

A lie is like a rampaging rhino,
charging no matter what.
A lie is like a scared monitor,
quick to attack when cornered.
A lie is like a ferocious fish
tearing the flesh off your bones.
A lie is like a venomous snake,
striking when danger is near.
A lie is like a savage cat,
ready to strike and ready to scratch.
A lie is like a crocodile
luring its prey.
A lie is like a monster mouse
nibbling away at you.
A lie is like a hippo
trying to overturn.
A lie is like a nightmare
crawling up your neck.
A lie is like quicksand
pulling you in.
A lie is like a boomerang,
it always comes back.

William Sherlock (11)
Mullion CP School

A LIE IS LIKE A . . .

A lie is like a weasel,
It will bite and never let go.

A lie is like a charging rhino,
It will never go away.

A lie is like an infectious disease
That affects everyone.

A lie is like a mosquito
Sucking the life out of you.

Thomas Bray (11)
Mullion CP School

A LIE

A lie is like a laughing hyena that hides the real truth.
A lie is like a whirlpool trying to suck you in.
A lie is like a lemon, sour and sweet.
A lie is like a cold that blocks you up inside.
A lie is like a hot brand that scars you for life.
A lie is like a voice at the back of your mind.
A lie is like a roller coaster taking your emotions up and down.
A lie is like a nightmare you never forget.
A lie is like a painting frozen in time.
A lie is like an eye keeping watch.

Robyn Rowarth (10)
Mullion CP School

CONFUSED?

There once was a train that gave green milk.
There once was a cow who liked to play football.
There once as a boy, fluffy and puffy.
There once was a cloud, noisy and fun.
There once as a party, icy and cold.
There once was a glacier, clever and cool.
There once was a teacher who fell off the rails.

Mathew Geach (11)
Mullion CP School

THERE ONCE...

There once was a horse called Syrinja
Who didn't like to linger,
We brought her back
To ride and hack,
She was bay not ginger.

With her little white feet
She was ever so neat,
Her tail so black
To show her tack,
Who you can never defeat.

Syrinja won four silvers and a gold
Two bronze that got old,
She could eat and eat
Her favourite was beet,
But then she got old.

Patricia Lepper (10)
Mullion CP School

A LIE

A lie
A lie is like
A lie is like a lemon
A lie is like a lemon, bitter and sharp.

A bully
A bully is like
A bully is like a buffalo
A bully is like a buffalo, boxing and bashing.

Andrew Greet (11)
Mullion CP School

THE GOALPOSTS

On the first day
only the goalposts watched the ball go through.

On the second day
only the goalposts noticed the free kick go in.

On the third day
only the goalposts heard the screaming of the foul.

On the final day
only the goalposts recognised they were alone.

Thomas Rendall (10)
Mullion CP School

A-J ANIMALS

A is for ants with big, red bums,
B is for baboons working all day,
C is for cats barking at the moon,
D is for dogs miaowing all day,
E is for elephants flapping in the water,
F is for fish baking in the mud,
G is for gorillas jumping around,
H is for hare swinging in a tree,
I is for iguana catching bugs,
J is for jaguar running really fast.

Yasmin Cottrell (10)
Mullion CP School

HYDRA

My scales are red and hard as diamonds,
My eyes shine like emeralds in the dim light of wooden torches,
I'm huge - bigger than other creatures.
Using my inferno to penetrate anything,
Then slash my enemies into dust
And not even a mark on my claws.
My claws are the size of knives, but ten times sharper
And don't forget my three heads
Equipped with bone-breaking jaws of steel.

Daniel Wilson (11)
Mullion CP School

FISHING

F   is for fish, too strong for your arms
I   is for 'I've got one Dad' as you bring a fish in
S   is for stirring ground bait, sticky and red
H   is for hauling a fish in smaller than you thought it was
I   is for icky as I cut out its guts
N   is for *now!* I've got a big one
G   is for getting wet as the giant fish splashes you with ice-cold water.

Cai Dale (11)
Mullion CP School

I WILL REMEMBER . . .

The swish of a curtain in a cool breeze,
The crunch of feet on the morning's frost,
The song of a bird always at ease,
The taste of chocolate and how much it costs.

And as my soul reaches the sun,
The way days finished, the way they'd begun,
The way I waved goodbye to the world.

      Then slipped away silently . . .

Sophie Enever (11)
Mullion CP School

THE SUPER 'S'

S is for sweatshirt, blue and baggy
S is for seesaw, rocking back and forth
S is for storm that blows you away
S is for shoe, spongy and light
S is for shooting, loud and deadly
S is for sad, sombre and sorry
S is for star, shiny and bright
S is for salami, spicy and yummy
S is for salad, crunchy and fun.

Joe Page (11)
Mullion CP School

THE SOLDIER

A nervous soldier searched for shelter,
The first blow came as a shock,
The second shot more accurate,
By the third he began to shiver
And steadily fell to the floor.
On the fourth, he saw nothing,
His mind, was blank.

David Cattran (10)
Mullion CP School

I Saw...

On Monday I saw a
blood-sucking elephant up in a tree.
On Tuesday I saw an
enormous, fat vampire drinking beer.
On Wednesday I saw a
cricket delivering post in London.
On Thursday I saw a
man eating a whale for tea.
On Friday I saw a
shark playing football for Man U.
On Saturday I saw a
lemon kicking a pip.
On Sunday I saw a
goatee horse shaving.
Now what can you see?

Lee Cattran (11)
Mullion CP School

Rainbow

Red, orange, yellow and green,
The rainbow is the biggest skipping rope
I've ever seen.

Blue, indigo and lastly violet
Are the weirdest colours
For an arched sky pilot.

Jon Lewis (11)
Mullion CP School

A Saw A ...

I saw an orange, flying through the air,
I saw a cricket ball, lying on the table,
I saw a book, tap dancing along the street,
I saw a man, wobbling high,
I saw a jelly, running through the town,
I saw a runner, writing on the board,
I saw a boy, flutter down,
I saw a leaf, warm and melting,
I saw a tub of ice cream, buzzing loudly,
I saw a Game Boy, playing sweet music,
I saw a tape, full of dark red wine,
I saw a big glass, bright and sunny,
I saw a postcard, flying high,
I saw a plane, breathing fire,
I saw a dragon, full of juice.

Ruth Oliver (10)
Mullion CP School

A Secret

A secret is like a treasure chest that should never be opened.
A secret is like a unicorn that nobody else should find.
A secret is like friendship that should never let go.
A secret is like a key that opens a door to the real wide world.
A secret is like a book that leads you to your destiny.
A secret is like an angel taking you up to Heaven.
A secret is like a sparkle shining like a star.
A secret is like a chain, if it breaks then it is lost forever.

Sarah Harding-Wilson (10)
Mullion CP School

MY MAGIC BOX

I will put in my box the sound of a wave
and a gentle, flowing river.
I will put in my box a Hungarian Horntail
as it awakens once again.
I will put in my box the flash of a wand
as the wizard shouts, 'Abara Kadabra!'
I will put in my box the Jabberwocky
as it horribly tears down Sherwood Forest.
I will put in my box the gentle sound
of the seaside on a beautiful day.

Nathan Davison (10)
Mullion CP School

THE WIND IS BURNING

Wind is one invisible ice cube
Wind is a cold hand closed over you
Wind is like your mum telling you to go to bed
Wind is like one big bad mood
Wind is like a sad film
Wind is like being in a fridge with a fan
Wind is like a spirit let loose
Wind is like a big nightmare
Wind is like a worrying wasp
Wind is like a rush of lava from the centre of the Earth
Wind is like being dead.

Harry Williams (10)
Nancledra CP School

A GREEN SQUIGGLE

A green squiggle
That makes you giggle
Hides in leaves
Dots like beads
Eight legs
A bit like pegs
A hard shell
That hangs on well
Then in spring
That tiny thing
Comes crawling out
Around and about
Huge wings
Pretty rings
It can fly oh so high

A butterfly.

Emily Becalick (9)
Nancledra CP School

THE TIN MINE

I attract tourists.
I am the silhouette on the hill.
I stand tall and straight.
When once I used to work
Now I stand wrecked.
I feel forgotten
And yet so many people know me.
I am pure Cornish
And I live on the moor.

Ella Frears Hogg (10)
Nancledra CP School

PASSENGER FLOATER

I sit tall and proud in the water.
I feel the sticky varnish being painted over me.
My name is on the side,
I want to show it off.
I am being surrounded by people gazing at me.
I feel proud as if I was a king.
I feel like an elephant at the zoo.
If the public want to see me, they have to pay.
Fishermen trust me.
I feel like I have to keep them safe.
I am sailing swiftly and beautifully away.

Alice Freeman (10)
Nancledra CP School

ADVERTISING

1970 teacher
Good condition
Bit grotty round the edges
Likes confiscating sledges
Runs on tea and biscuits
Come around, just don't miss it
Will swap for teenage male
Who likes Boddies, lager and ale.

Chris Lanyon (11)
Nancledra CP School

IN THE BOAT

In the boat
was a coated float.
The shark wobbled it with a strike
the boat had a hole on its right.
I found a leak in the boat
it was almost full.
The dolphin came up
with some diamonds and pearls.
The boat came down
with all the weight.
The men fell out, what was their fate?
The dolphin saved the men
and brought them ashore.
The killer whale came up
and helped the dolphin some more.

Charlie Goodchild (9)
Nanpean CP School

HIDDEN TREASURE

The pirates were sailing over the sea
And searching for the treasures that belonged to me.
The pirates reached the sand
And thought they heard a bang.
But with a crash and a bang
The whale shark sang.
The sea horse came
With a brother and sister the same.
At last the pirates found it
With something strange in it, just a bit!

Tamsyn Fulbrook (10)
Nanpean CP School

HIDDEN TREASURE

On we sail, on we sail
On we sail finding treasure
On we sail through the darkness
And reach an island with so much pleasure.

We entered the palace
With a bright red door
We saw someone poor
We found a door
Leading to the treasure
And then we had so much pleasure.

We went inside and picked up the chest
Then we opened it
What a journey
I'd love to do that again!

Laura Hampton (10)
Nanpean CP School

JACK'S ADVENTURE

There once was a boy called Jack,
Who had a potato sack.
He drank from a fountain,
Then climbed a mountain
And got booted off by a yak!

There once was a great big yak,
Who booted off Jack.
He slid down the mountain,
Went into the fountain
And got attacked by the potato sack.

Aaron Fowler (10)
Nanpean CP School

HIDDEN TREASURES

In a castle, while it was dark,
Everyone was asleep, as I followed my path.
The staircase led to an old wooden door,
Then I saw a little trapdoor in the floor.

I followed it down, it led a long way,
When at last I saw, it had changed to day,
As I carefully climbed out of the hole,
I felt as if I was a little mole.

As I brushed the sand off me,
I looked around, pirates were staring at me,
Then they made some hard chains out of some wire.

'We must find those treasures,' I heard one say last night,
And all of a sudden we all had a fight,
Because I wanted to find them I said
I had hit three of them on the head.

I left at midnight so I could find
The treasure chest that had been designed.
To my surprise I found a map,
I read it while it was on my lap.

On it there was a cross,
For the treasure that was across,
Left a bit,
Down a bit,
Into the bottom of the sea,
To my surprise,
I saw with my eyes,
A treasure chest waiting for me.

Samantha Marshall (9)
Nanpean CP School

HIDDEN TREASURE

I was climbing up a tree
Then walking across the sea
I was looking for the treasure chest
For lucky, lucky me.

It wasn't to be, standing next to me
The wizard of the sea
Appeared upon the sand
Stood with a magic wand in his large hand.

I saw him point at me
Then say, 'Come to me.'
I stood in fear
He had a grin ear to ear
I walked in steps
Then he leapt to me
I cannot see!

Joanne Knowles (9)
Nanpean CP School

HIDDEN TREASURES

The pirates were sailing over the sea
And searching for the treasures that belong to me.
The pirates reached the sand
And thought they heard a band.
The tooth shark sang
And the pirates heard a bang.
The octopus came
With a family the same.
The pirates grabbed the treasure
For their pleasure.

Kirsty Burford (10)
Nanpean CP School

HIDDEN TREASURE

Oh, we're going down to the beach today,
We will have to drive a very long way.
We'll have a picnic on the sand,
Oh, won't it be so very grand.

We go down under the sea,
With all the sea creatures and me.
I found a shipwrecked boat
That had a little float.

As I entered I did find
A treasure chest that had been designed.
As I carefully opened the chest
It was so hard I had a rest.
Then I saw the gold so shiny
When I reached the surface
My friends all said, 'Blimey.'

Jade Stephens (9)
Nanpean CP School

HIDDEN TREASURES

I am in the desert all alone
It's not much fun on my own.
Exploring through the dusty sand
Standing on the yellow land.
Suddenly I see someone in the distance having fun
And someone lying in the sun.
Aren't they the lucky ones
But where's the hidden treasure?

Katy Philp (10)
Nanpean CP School

HIDDEN TREASURE

I don't want to be a footballer
because I don't like getting muddy.
When I get muddy
it turns out to be a tragedy.
When someone tackles me
my tongue goes crackly.
My football boots are muddy
so that is a tragedy.

I want to find the treasure
because it will give me so much pleasure.
I want to find the treasure.
I got what I wanted and so
I bought everything in the shops
and made my life a better thing.

Sean Hambly (9)
Nanpean CP School

HIDDEN TREASURE

There was an old man who liked to play pass the parcel
Who walked along a very big castle
Who found a map
And gave himself a slap.

He found some treasure
Thought he'd have the pleasure,
He went home
And bought a dome.

Joseph Hawes (10)
Nanpean CP School

INVASION

'Daddy, I want to come, I really want to go.'
'No son, no, no, no.'
'Why Dad? Why?'
'The time is not nigh.'

Bows and arrows fire away
But suddenly I hear Dad say,
'They've got weapons superior to us!'

Suddenly the line goes dead,
Dad takes a bullet to the head,
Not unforeseen, his life's not wasted.

'Hello Dad!'
'I'm back my son.'
'How did it go? I hope it was fun.'
'Now listen son, don't lie to me,
You watched it all on our TV.'

'OK Dad, but you did bad,
It really did make me sad
To see you get in such a fix,
You didn't eat your Weetabix!'

'I'm sorry Dad, but you did bad,
I thought that you would take over Earth
Just like you did with planet Perth.
I don't think you should have written that letter,
It just made it all much better
For them to prepare that huge gun,
I bet they had a lot of fun!'
      Sorry Earth!

Zackary Such (10)
Penponds School

MORDOR

In a place called Mordor,
Where the ring was made,
All the light in the hills
Had started to fade.

The Orcs were dug up,
Those ugly things
And the ring that was made,
Was named The Lord Of The Ring.

It overpowered the rings,
The 19 changed bad,
It turned the kings crazy,
It turned the kings mad.

The kings who turned crazy,
They rode to Mount Doom,
Going faster and faster,
Riding into the gloom.

Then they hear Gollum,
Gollum's poor cry,
He's being tortured,
They think he might die.

The kings were now knights,
With huge devilish claws,
They wore black cloaks
And fought in many wars.

So if the ring was not destroyed,
Middle Earth would end,
And only where the ring was made,
It only would then bend.

So if little Frodo Baggins had not destroyed the ring,
The madness would start a combat,
Overwhelm the power,
The power of The Lord Of The Rings.

Samuel Jones (11)
Penponds School

LITTLE DROPLET

The rain is drifting softly, gently,
A droplet fell on my head,
As it is falling it cracks its shell
And unleashes its cold pain,
It tickles my nose.
My feet are sore,
As I lie on the frosty pavement,
My stomach hungry,
All over my body are goosebumps,
On the palms of my hands blisters,
My home is a cardboard box.
Getting moved on from the bus station,
Again.
Doesn't anyone care?
I'm all alone in the world.
I wish every night for a warm bed,
But my home is just a forest full of pain.
My whole body is shaking,
As Christmas Day ends
And night comes,
So the stars are my light
And my only friend in the universe.

Hanna-Marie Creese (11)
Penponds School

Moonlight

Night is my favourite time of day,
Especially when the silver moonlight
Shines on the bottom of my bed.
I can spend hours at night,
Looking at the moon through my telescope.
The moon looks better with the stars twinkling.
The blackened sky changes colour
From a black to a dark blue.
It keeps changing, never the same,
Until the moon goes down and the sun comes up.
Tonight I'm camping in my tent and
I can see the silver of the moon
Shining through the canvas.
I can hear the owl and owlet talking.
I can smell the scent of dew
Forming on the lonely grass.
I can touch the twinkling in the dark vastness of space.

Emma Bingham (10)
Penponds School

The Wind

I blow through the trees and scare you out of your wits.
I make the noise at night that makes you go into your mum and dad's
                                                                                room.
I squeal and scream from the dark sky.
I see a wolf. Shall I blow him over? But no.
I am strong, I can blow over a tree.
I play with the stars in the dark sky.
Ooooooo
I go past the window.

Michael Cowley (11)
Penponds School

TWENTY MINUTES AND FOURTEEN SECONDS

Twenty minutes and fourteen seconds till home time,
Pinnggg the bells rang at last,
I wonder what homework is tonight,
Maths, science or reading?

I just want to go and watch TV
But oh no I have to do my homework,
I am going to miss the Ghost Hunter.

Will they find out who the person is?
At last I am going to sleep,
I thing I am dreaming about it,
Ahhh! I've woken up, I've missed who the person was.

Melodie Jade Such (8)
Penponds School

SCHOOL

I like having a play time.
I like painting a picture.
Ka boom, ka boom, ka boom.
I like having to work.
I like writing.
Ka bam, ka bam, ka bam.
I like helping people.
I like reading books.
Ka bum, ka bum, ka bum.
I like drawing a picture.
I like thinking too.
Ka boom, ka boom, ka boom.

Christopher Quigley (9)
Penponds School

WHERE'S MY JUMPER?

I get up to have my breakfast,
Juice, toast, cereal.
I go to get changed into my school clothes,
T-shirt, skirt, jumper, tights.

I put on my tights,
Skirt and T-shirt.
But where's my jumper?
Mystery, mystery, mystery.

Ollie's got his jumper
And his trousers.
Hold on a minute,
He's got two jumpers.

He's got a big grin
On his face, face, face.
He's got me into so much
Trouble, trouble, trouble.

I walk down the
Stairs, stairs, stairs.
Will I, will I not,
Will I get into trouble?

Elizabeth Nidds (10)
Penponds School

DRAGON

Awake all day, all night,
Guarding treasure stolen long ago,
Many brave knights have tried to get but failed,
The wrath of dragon, dragon, dragon.

Awake all day, all night,
In a horrible cave,
Hungry, bloodthirsty and painful
Job for a dragon, dragon, dragon.

Shay McCauley-Dawes (9)
Penponds School

MORNING

I get up out of bed
On a summer's morning
And open my window
And watch the sun
Rising into the sky.

I listen to the birds
Singing sweetly
High in the trees.
The warm, gentle breeze
Scattering leaves and twigs
On the ground.

The trees swaying as
The breeze passes by.
The shiny fish swimming
In the warm, clear water.

The bright colours of flowers,
The smell of the honeysuckle
Fills the air.
It makes me feel joyful.

Gemma McCormick (9)
Penponds School

DEATH IS YOUR GIFT

Screaming from her corner,
She cried
As the bloody dagger hit her heart.
She curled up, her vision faded
And for a second time he hit her
Until she had only strength
For this last word of revenge.

His red, fiery eyes daggered hers
And for a third time he hit her,
And just kept staring.
She had no strength to scream,
She could only cry.
She just lay there and cried
And for a fourth time he hit her.

It was getting very dark now,
All she could see were his eyes staring.
She felt helpless.
She said to herself,
'I'm going to die here.'

Elinor Weedon (10)
Penponds School

THE OWL

It's evening time,
No school left,
I look out the window,
Is the owl sleeping?

Then I did a roll and a blade
Down the hill,
A glide and a slide
And fall over backwards.

It's night-time,
Time for bed,
The hooting of the owl,
Keeps me awake all night.

And the silent night
As I creep downstairs,
No noise but the hooting of the owl.
Where did it all go? I asked myself in wonder.

Bethan Pugh (10)
Penponds School

CANYON

Walking through the canyon,
In a summer morning breeze,
Looking up and down
At the light brown leaves.

Big, tall cliffs
And cacti too,
Gunshots by the minute,
Oooooohhhhh!

Walking through the canyon,
I look up in the sky,
I see an eagle soaring by,
His coloured wings way up in the sky.

As I walk back to my tent,
I feel the wind on the back of my neck,
The eagle is still soaring high,
Until the break of day does die.

Lauren Battershill (10)
Penponds School

OUR CAT

We go out to party,
Leaving our cat on the sofa.
I bet he won't be there long,
I can just imagine it now,
Him inviting all of his friends over.

We're just getting into the swing,
I bet he's doing the same,
Up over the wall they'll be going,
To join him in his fame.

We're on the karaoke,
I bet he's up on the garden wall
With all of his mates,
Singing the cats' chorus call.

It's time to go, it's time for bed,
So we all get tucked up
Because we're sleepyheads.
So off to sleep till morning comes
And that's when his life begins.

Emma Rowe (9)
Penponds School

WHICH WAY?

Which way to go?
Which way to go?
Where the wolf howls or where the birds sing!

Which way to go?
Which way to go?
Where the wind blows hard or to the sunny day!

Which way to go?
Which way to go?
Where children scream in terror or where
                    children laugh and play!

Nobody knows which way to go,
What to do or where!

Charlotte Wandless (10)
Penponds School

THE BEACH AT DAWN

She's on the beach before seven,
The cold and mist means nothing to her.
Walking with sand between her toes
And sandals in her hand.

The sea is calm and still,
There is peacefulness.
Seabirds flying above her,
Squawking and talking loudly.

She sees people in the distance,
People on the cliffs.
The little waves from the rock pools,
With marine life swimming in them.

It is now seven o'clock
And the sky is starting to change.
All the people have gone,
She is the only person left to see the sun break the horizon.

Rosanna Roberts (10)
Penponds School

ANGELS DO NOT MIX WITH SCHOOL WORK

The angel comes to school with the little boy,
But the angel hasn't a clue what to do.
The boy is asking the angel what to do with his work,
But the angel hasn't got a clue what to do.

The boy and the angel are walking to lunch,
The boy is asking the angel what to do
But the angel hasn't a clue what to do.

Home time, the boy is asking the angel to help him pack his bag,
But the angel hasn't got a clue what to do.
Bedtime, the boy is asking the angel to help him get ready for bed,
But the angel hasn't got a clue what to do.
The boy is never alone.

Joe Weeks (10)
Penponds School

A DAY AT FLAMBARDS

I went on the Thunderbolt but I felt a little sick,
and then I went on the roller coaster and nearly fell off.
So I went on the log flume but I nearly drowned,
I went on the Space Mission but my head nearly came off,
and I went on Shiver Me Timbers and was frozen,
I went to the funfair to have some fun,
It's time to go home,
Oh no, look out,
We are going to crash!

Thomas Heywood (9)
Penponds School

THE BIRDS AT NIGHT

The sunset calls us, we go up
                to the trees to watch
The orange and yellow picture move
                down the mountain.

The silver circle rises, stars come
                out to play
We all want to get home to our
                blanket of straw.

The squeals of the wind is like a little girl
                crying for her mum
We glide through the midsummer night air
                like a kite.

The horses run wild down there
                it's like
Shooting stars on the ground
                we want to get home.

The night light has always
                been there
Do we really need to get home?

The silver circle goes down
                stars go away
We go up to the trees to watch the yellow and gold picture
                crawl up the mountain.

Kelly Symons (10)
Penponds School

CATS

I was having a lovely supper,
I finished my supper, I was getting sleepy,
The moon was shining on the mat,
I fell asleep.

I had the most peculiar dream,
I dreamt that I was in love with a mouse.
I woke up and screamed,
My eyes were like crystals,
I washed myself,
My tail was flicking furiously.

I visited the art gallery,
Everything was still wet.
Paint dripped onto my thick, white coat,
Wool tangled me up,
I pulled and pulled,
Suddenly I spotted Emma Jam Pot,
She screamed, her face went red.

She went for me,
I ran for it,
I rolled in the carpet,
I got tangled up even more
With wool dragging behind me,
Somehow the carpet changed colour.

Abi Skewes (10)
Penponds School

SUNRISE SURPRISE

Rays of light shone through the curtains,
I stretched and gave a yawn,
Realised that it was a summer's day
And dashed out to see the dawn.

The sun was like a big, bright orange,
Rising in the east,
I could hear the baby birds chirping,
As they had their morning feast.

Blackbirds were tapping on the ground for worms,
While slugs and snails slithered round,
The songbird sang its joyful song
As it fluttered to the ground.

The dewdrops glistened like crystals,
They sparkled until noon,
The petals opened peacefully
As the bumblebees hummed their tune.

The trees swayed in the morning breeze
As a butterfly flew past me,
With its bright and beautiful wings
The colour of the sea.
What a sunrise surprise!

Tamsyn Allen (10)
Penponds School

Me

My smelly, cheesy feet sweat when I run.
My brown eyes gaze at football.
My apple-shaped head holds a brain inside me.
My long arms are stretchy elastic bands.

My hidden treasures inside me are . . .
My brain that keeps me working.
My heart that pumps blood through my body.
My bones that keep me standing.
My muscles that hold my veins and bones.
My legs that let me walk.
My small teeth are as white as my bones.

My hidden treasures are . . .
The shiny green leaves growing on a massive tree.
The old tumbling brown leaves falling off.
The flowers popping up from the earth's floor.
The little bright red thorns growing out of a green bush.

Gavin Parker (7)
Perranporth CP School

All About Myself

My outsideness is . . .
Gigantic legs for kicking footballs and skateboarding and running.
My sea blue eyes tracking down everything I come across.

My hidden treasures are . . .
My booming brain ticking.
My active skeleton ready to rumble any second.
My flexible back bending for England.

Ted Allsop (8)
Perranporth CP School

THE LOST WORLD

My outsideness is . . .
My glowing eyes piercing in the dark.
My hidden treasure is . . . my wobbly white, stiff, lazy skeleton.
My outsideness is . . . my tousled head as hard as a solid rock.
My hidden treasure is . . . my veins sucking blood through my body
and back to my heart.

Adrian Hennuyer (8)
Perranporth CP School

MY HIDDEN TREASURES

My outsideness is . . .
My strong hands grasping a football.
My terrific leg booting a football across a field.
My sea-blue eyes glowing in the night.
My hidden treasure is my strong, kind heart
pumping blood around my brilliant body.

Ryan Barnes (8)
Perranporth CP School

MY HIDDEN TREASURES

My eyes like shimmering marbles.
My hair is golden thread.
My hidden treasures are . . .
My mum,
My memory of my grandad makes me happy.
The kindness and smile in my heart.

Ellie-Jae Lewis (8)
Perranporth CP School

MY TREASURES

My outsideness is . . .
My little mask of freckles.
My straining, short arms trying to reach the cupboard doors.

My hidden treasures are . . .
My friendship, kindness and happiness.
The daffodils in spring.
Rainbows with warm colours.
Sounds of the sea.
Joy with my friends in the playground.
The cold blowing of the wind.
Crystal hailstones tapping against bedroom windows.
Buzzing of bees in summertime.
Cold snowmen in the corners of winter parks.
The bare trees with flowing leaves.
Gently stroking the ground.
Beating drums in the parade.

Abigail Brandreth (8)
Perranporth CP School

POEM WORLD

My hidden treasures inside are . . .
Watering trees and plants,
Caring for puppies and kittens,
Riding a horse,
Climbing rocks on the beach
The promise of God
Crying in the wind.

Amy Voyce (7)
Perranporth CP School

HAPPINESS

My outsideness is . . . my little mask of freckles.
My outsideness is . . . the talking mouth that never stops.
My outsideness is . . . the long, running legs, leaping around in the air.
My outsideness is . . . the heart pumping my working body.
My insideness is . . . the ballet legs dancing to the music.
My hidden treasures is . . . my beautiful butterfly smile making
                                             other people happy too.
My hidden treasures is . . . the caring friendship of friends.
My hidden treasure is . . . the daffodils in the spring making me happy.
My hidden treasure is . . . the blue sea sparkling in the summer.
My hidden treasure is . . . the falling snow in winter making me sleepy.
My hidden treasure is . . . my colourful rainbow of kindness.

Lucy Rickett (7)
Perranporth CP School

THE LOST RAINBOW

The lost rainbow sees my outsideness . . .
My silky, shiny hair that swishes in the strong wind.
My dark, chocolate eyes scan my friends.
My endless legs grow and grow.

The rainbow sees my hidden treasures . . .
A soft smile from my heart.
My flexible back.
A heart that pounces up and down again and again.
My talented computer brain always working.
The powerful, colourful rainbow that sparkles in the sun while
                                                  watching me.

Karina Davis (8)
Perranporth CP School

HIDDEN TREASURES

My outsideness is . . .
My mask of freckles.
My balloon-shaped head.
My butterfly eyelashes.
My cherry cheeks.
My blueberry eyes.

My hidden treasure is . . .
The crystal that is gold in the sun.
The wagging tails of puppy dogs.
The pattering of the dice rolling across the table.
The jumping of the deer.
The clickety-clackety of the train going over the bridge.
The sunset relaxing on the ocean.
The light of my friendship.

Jannah-Beth Lucas (7)
Perranporth CP School

HIDDEN TREASURES

My outsideness is . . .
My dark chocolate eyes.
My strong legs booting a football in to the goal.
My legs are 66cm long.
My head is like a football.
My hair sticks up like a porcupine.

My hidden treasures are . . .
My mum and dad.
My brain clunking away.
My heart pumping the blood around me.

Joshua Hider (9)
Perranporth CP School

MY HIDDEN HEART

My round conker face.
My flexible body.
My bendy legs.
My sharpened nose.
My cheesy feet and
My jelly belly!

My hidden treasure is . . .
My ticking brain.
My straining bones.
My streaming blood, flowing through my veins.
My loving heart beating like a drum.
My mum and dad so special to me.
My nan's funny way of speaking.
My sister helping me.

Georgina Musselwhite (8)
Perranporth CP School

INSIDENESS AND OUTSIDENESS

My outsideness is . . .
My chocolate brown eyes are as small as stones,
                        are brilliant book readers.
My loving smile shining like the sun.
I'm tall and flexible.

My hidden treasures are . . .
My insideness is
My computer brain, talented on the PlayStation.
My heart inside me pumping and loving.

Joseph Miller (6)
Perranporth CP School

BEST SECRETS

My ruler legs snap when I bend them,
My beady arms are like strings of golden jewels.
My woolly wiry hair blows in the wind.
My hidden heart is covered in duvets.
My brain is like a pumping heater.
A beautiful garden inside is my body.
Friendship fairies glimmer.

Emily Horrigan (8)
Perranporth CP School

A MAGICAL FACTORY

If I owned a magical factory . . .
I would make a clear swimming pool out of blue blood.
I would make coloured quill pens out of a short rainbow.
I would make a copy of me out of lime-green diamonds.
I would make a brilliant sun out of a round light bulb.
I would make a fat house out of £50 notes.
I would make a comfy bed out of fluffy wool.
I would make a small song out of a long opera.
I would make a large school out of best Belgian chocolate.
I would make a mad teacher out of crashed computers.
I would make a pod of dolphins out of green seaweed.
I would make spicy spaghetti out of wriggling worms.
I would make a speedy tortoise out of a slimy egg.
I would make a special friend out of bread and butter.
I would make a chocolate finger out of a tall tree.
I would make a rhyming poem out of sweet singing mermaids.

Jessica May Palmer (11)
Polruan CP School

IF I OWNED...

If I owned a magical factory -

I would make a white computer out of papier mâché.
I would make a jacuzzi bath out of orange sponges.
I would make an uncomfortable bed out of sticky glue.
I would make a soggy cereal out of a banana skin.
I would make a blood-flavoured ice cream out of red wine.
I would make a statue of me out of a chocolate mousse.
I would make a Flubber ball out of black tarmac.
I would make a colouring book out of mouldy peanuts.
I would make an old magic wand out of soapy bubbles.
I would make the fastest broomstick ever out of slimy seaweed.
I would make a gold watch out of running water!

Joseph Tomlin (9)
Polruan CP School

IF I OWNED...

If I owned a magical factory . . .

I would make a duplicate of me out of clinging seaweed.
I would make a solid gold fountain pen out of live plastic.
I would make a stopwatch out of melting ice.
I would make thatched top hats out of deep-mined coal.
I would make a troll's mace out of bone china.
I would make a flashy speedboat out of powder tablets.
I would make an extinct volcano out of a wet tissue.
I would make a football book out of jelly castles.

Mathew Beresford (10)
Polruan CP School

IF I OWNED...

If I owned a magical factory -

I would make twirling spaghetti out of Easter egg chocolate.
I would make sharp rocks out of squidgy jelly.
I would make Lego bricks out of chocolate sauce.
I would make a large grandfather clock out of rushing water.
I would make a red stopwatch out of salt and vinegar crisp.
I would make a bald man out of crunch chips.
I would make a red frog out of a roaring lion.
I would make a primary teacher out of a block of clay.
I would make a newsagents shop out of melting chocolate.
I would make a championship motorbike out of curry Pot Noodles.
I would make a speedy skateboard out of a leaping salmon.
I would make a banana milkshake out of muddy water.
I would make a Harry Potter book out of milk bottle tops.
I would make a tall tree out of clear ice!

Tom Nutland (11)
Polruan CP School

IF I OWNED...

If I owned a magical factory -

I would make priceless caviar out of sticky mud.
I would make Game Boy Advance out of shiny steel.
I would make a tumbledown house out of chocolate.
I would make a cool robot out of hot soup.
I would make a moody teacher out of silly clay.
I would make a moving boat out of hard bricks.
I would make a luminous UFO out of strong wine.

I would make a jumping skateboard out of clear glass.
I would make a backpack out of yesterday's newspaper.
I would make Hogwart's School out of strawberry jelly.
I would make a swimming bird out of hairy hair.
I would make a match football out of fierce fire.
I would make a David Beckham out of premier goalposts.
I would make a referee's whistle out of seagulls' feathers.
I would make bright stars out of mouldy cheese.

Rhys Lamy (11)
Polruan CP School

IF I OWNED...

If I owned a magical factory -

I would make colourful pens out of an arched rainbow.
I would make a cuddly bear out of nimbus clouds.
I would make a cartoon character out of sun-yellow paint.
I would make a body spray out of rotten garlic.
I would make a crying doll out of drops of rain.
I would make an upright sunflower out of an oak tree.
I would make a sugary doughnut out of bumpy rocks.
I would make a buzzing fly out of flat pancakes.
I would make sloppy spaghetti out of wiggly worms.
I would make a knight's sword out of jumping fish.
I would make a mechanic's spanner out of a fierce crab.
I would make a primary school out of desert sand.
I would make a barking dog out of pink ham.
I would make an English teacher out of a chattering parrot.
I would make the spinning world out of sweet candyfloss.

Jasmine Libby (10)
Polruan CP School

IF I OWNED...

If I owned a magical factory...

I would make some fat bacon out of tissue paper.
I would make a fluffy dog out of oak wood.
I would make a bouncy bed out of lunch boxes.
I would make an educational computer out of black leather.
I would make a sharp dart out of cool jeans.
I would make some white paper out of a plastic door.
I would make a thin worm out of a wooden pencil.
I would make a red car out of mashed potato.
I would make a rag doll out of thin carpet.
I would make a wooden bookshelf out of dogs' bones.
I would make a creeping plant out of plastic CD cases.
I would make a rocking chair out of seagull feathers.
I would make an oblong book out of piano keys.
I would make a blackboard out of coloured paper.
I would make an old grandfather clock out of orange pillowcases!

Emma Nutty (9)
Polruan CP School

DANIEL'S HIDDEN TREASURES

They live way out of reach,
They light up like a bushbaby's eyes,
They are a wonder to our eyes,
Not always do they appear as if they are a shy baby,
They only disappear when the sun rises,
The only other object that shines like them would be the silver moon,
They look down on us like a swooping owl to a lemming,
You might not have guessed yet but these things that I describe
                                            are the shining stars.

Daniel Warden (11)
St Breaca CE Primary School, Helston

KENNING

I can hold your biggest dream or your most feared nightmare.
If you want adventure, just knock on my door and I will open.
I am rectangular.
I have leaves but they don't fall off in autumn.
I can be your most prized possession or thrown under a bunk-bed
                                                         and forgotten.
I have no arms or legs.
I have no other bones but I have a spine.
I am not independent like a cat and I don't like to go in water.
I have two worms lying inside me.
What am I?

Ben Powell (10)
St Breaca CE Primary School, Helston

MY SPECIAL PLACE

My secret place is special,
It's hidden far away;
A place where I can laugh or cry,
A place where I can play.

My place is safe from monsters,
Trapped in the wilderness;
But if I wondered out of it,
I would be in a mess.

All this weird fantasy,
Is just inside my head;
The reality of my special place,
Is only my cosy bed!

Juliet Robertson (9)
St Breaca CE Primary School, Helston

PIRATE'S GOLD

P irate's gold is shimmering steel,
I ts dull eyes copper in the summer sun,
R eally ancient jewels getting shown in the dusty museum,
A ll the chattering tourists come to stare,
T hink about wicked pirates long, long ago,
E nding, dead for protecting their gold.

Michael Worden (10)
St Breaca CE Primary School, Helston

HIDDEN TREASURE

The sky is like hidden treasure.
Some fluffy clouds,
A bright shiny sun,
A soft white moon
Sprinkled with glittery stars,
Violet blue, lilac blue.
The sky is like hidden treasure.

Georgia Harrison & Charlotte Wells (9)
St Breaca CE Primary School, Helston

GINGER

I have golden amber eyes.
Occasionally I can be wise.
My name and coat is Ginger.
I like to go outside and linger.
I think I'm richer than others
Although I have no sister or brothers.
Where did I hide that treasure?
I hid it at my leisure.

Georgina Wells (10)
St Breaca CE Primary School, Helston

NATURE'S TREASURE

My treasure is up on an emerald hill,
And with peridot ferns swaying beside it,
Opal clouds fly by casting dark shadows on its branches,
The sound of golden buzzards crying in the cool air,
Its bronze trunk firmly set in the lose soil,
Its leaves left years ago,
My treasure is up on an emerald hill.

Rosie Woodman (11)
St Breaca CE Primary School, Helston

KENNING

She lives in the sea,
She loves to eat fish,
Her silky blue skin,
Is like the misty mist,
Her fin is as spiky as a pin,
My animal is a dolphin!

Rosie Reynolds & Chloe (10)
St Breaca CE Primary School, Helston

KENNING

I am a multicoloured line!
I reach from high mountains to high mountains!
Sometimes I have a reflection!
I am a bright arch but I'm not a bow!
Normally I live in rain but need the sun to shine!
I line right up high in the sky!
Apparently at either end I have a bright pot of gold?
What am I?

Jessica Harrison (10)
St Breaca CE Primary School, Helston

FOOTBALL PLAYERS

Figo, World Player of the Year.
Okacha, Nigerian midfielder.
Owen, European Footballer of the Year.
Toldo, Argentinean keeper.
Beckham, fantastic free kick taker.
Aldair, Brazilian centre back.
Ljungberg, redhead Swede.
Litmanen, Liverpool, midfielder.
Pele, legend footballer.
Lizarazu, French centre back.
Anelka, Liverpool striker.
Young, anonymous footballer.
Eusebio, another legend footballer.
Rivaldo, Barcelona footballer.
Zidane, best footballer *ever!*

Ben Watters (9) & Perry Ware (10)
St Breaca CE Primary School, Helston

MY DIARY

S hiny in the light,
E very single day,
C ast a glimpse,
R ead aloud,
E ven you can't tell it's
T otally secret.

D o you dare to go in there?
I n it my total secrets,
A nd dates,
R eady for the
Y ear.

Ailsa Sutherland (9)
St Breaca CE Primary School, Helston

HIDDEN TREASURE

I point out birds for my master so I get them for my supper.
I could be big or small, maybe in-between.
I chase off animals that pursue birds because they get on my nerves.
I am a ky which is Cornish for what I am.
Some people love me with all their hearts, love and strength.
I'm a treasure to children and my master,
But just another mouth to feed to grown-ups.
I'm not going to tell you what I am,
So you'll have to guess!

Merryn Tresidder (9) & Michael Hall (11)
St Breaca CE Primary School, Helston

SQUIDJEREE

If you go the bottom of the sea,
You might find the Squidjeree.
It has no fin,
It has no tail
But it smells!
It has no colour,
It has no predator
And can't be killed.
It's peaceful and harmless
It has no gills.
So if you go to the bottom of the sea
You might just find the Squidjeree!

Felix Lovell (9) & Sam Ratcliffe (10)
St Breaca CE Primary School, Helston

MY SECRET PLACE

My favourite space,
Is a wonderful place,
I like it so much,
It's so soft to touch,
Doesn't make a sound,
Great fun all round,
Sometimes needs dusting,
Doesn't need a broom,
For my favourite place is my *bedroom*.

Gemma Reid (9)
St Breaca CE Primary School, Helston

WINTER POEM

Golden blanket crystal, wrapped up in bed.
When he fell asleep,
Jack Frost came to his head
To turn him into ice so deep.

In the morning ice could be seen.
He got out silently
And jumped downstairs,
With his silver clothes iced frozen there.

Out of the bottom window he stood,
Jack Frost out there
In the backyard,
Watching his dead heart hard.

'I caught you boy,' Jack said.
He lifted his deadly hand,
And he laughed
Like a frosty man.

Marcus Lukacs (8)
St Columb Major CP School

EMMA

Emma is my best friend,
She pulls funny faces.
Emma is my best friend,
We go to lovely places.

Emma is my best friend,
We like to play outside.
Emma is my best friend,
We search far and wide.

Emma is my best friend
As maybe you can see.
Emma is my best friend,
She tells jokes to me.

Emma is my best friend,
To each other, letters we send.
Emma is my best friend,
Our friendship will never end!

Carly Rundle (9)
St Columb Major CP School

NIGHT

In my bedroom it is quiet like an empty church.
The trees are rustling and tapping on the window like
Someone trying to get in.
The street light is a giant with his torch shining on my bed.
Outside my room a deserted garden like a black carpet.
The clock ticks like an unexploded bomb.
The lightning is a disco light flashing in the school hall.

Jenna Rundle (11)
St Columb Major CP School

WINTER POEM

Windy, cold,
Shimmering gold
And now
Glittering white clouds
Dancing around.

Dark as dawn
Snowflakes fall,
Look outside
There's a
Thundering storm.

Snow can fall,
Look, see
The animals
Sleeping, cosy,
Like a person.

Think
Of the sad people,
Icy and frozen.
Think of wet
And of cold.

Millie Norris (8)
St Columb Major CP School

THE ZOO

At the zoo, I have so much fun,
Playing with the animals and everyone.
I like the monkeys, they are sweet,
But the snakes, they slide all over my feet.

The tigers and the lions too,
I like them, do you?
So go to the zoo, you'll have so much fun,
Playing with the animals and everyone.

Jodi Aldridge (10)
St Columb Major CP School

WINTER

Winter feels like
I'm trapped inside an icicle.
Silver ice is determined
To make me slip.
Jack Frost creeps around my garden
And freezes me to the bone.

Thoughtless children
Out in T-shirts,
Freezing themselves to death.
Animals hibernate
As the cruel winter flows by.
Wood burning, fires for warmth.

Flowers die out,
Winter cold, freezing.
But one thing about winter
It's nearly over,
Waiting,
Waiting for the spring.

Rachel Batchelor (8)
St Columb Major CP School

My Rabbits

I have three rabbits called
Cottontail, Claire and Spot.
Spot is as cute as a baby
Sleeping in a cot.
Claire out of all the rabbits
Is the only one with bad habits.
Cottontail is very quiet
While the other two are causing a riot.
I like my rabbits very much,
They're nice and soft to touch.
All my rabbits have habits,
But I like them all the same.
That's my rabbits.

Nicole Braden (9)
St Columb Major CP School

Families

Families are important,
Families help you,
They're always there for you,
Families help you when you're younger,
Families help you when you're older,
Families are important,
Families help you with your homework,
Don't you see . . .
Families are lovely.

Charlotte Sztajneet (8)
St Columb Major CP School

SHIVERING WHITE

The man shivers like ice in clothes,
But he doesn't have clothes . . . it's snow.
Hair so white, and cloth so white too,
But what on earth does he do?

I like to run in the snow at night,
I peep outside my window,
I see the little man sometimes
But this night snow comes in . . .

When I wake in the morning
A knock sounds on my window,
In the white garden a man,
As white as the snow.

Korrie Hegarty (8)
St Columb Major CP School

MY FAMILY

My dad tells me off when I'm bad,
He sometimes makes me very sad.
My mum sends me to my room with a big *boom!*
My sister is full of fun,
And she gobbles up a big icy bun.
My cat, Dinky likes to explore
Inside, outside and many places more.
My other cat is big and chubby
And she's my sister's best buddy.

Aimee Passmore (9)
St Columb Major CP School

MY FAMILY

My soft black and white cat Toby,
My brother Martin who is artistic but sometimes annoying,
Mum who is kind and generous and a good cook,
Dad is soft and cares a lot,
Grandma is the best,
She knits and dresses my doll, Holly,
Grandad is the best too . . .
Then me, the youngest in the house.

Natalie Pearce (10)
St Columb Major CP School

SPIDERS

Spiders are like black balls of string,
They are like eight pieces of spaghetti.
They look like mini Maltesers.
Their webs are like stretchy elastic bands,
So next time you see a spider look carefully,
What do you see?

Joanna Powell (10)
St Columb Major CP School

ANIMALS

All different kinds of animals
From lots of ants to a big elephant
That eats plants.
Caterpillars *munch, munch*
Leaves for their lunch.
That's animals!

Caitlin Baker (9)
St Columb Major CP School

WHAT IS THE MOON?

The moon is a golf ball swung up in the sky.
The moon is a boat on the mirrored surface.
The moon is a round lump of cheese.
The moon is a silver eye of a needle.
The moon has an outline like a shadow edge.
The moon is a bead in the blackness of the night.
The moon is a balloon and when it becomes morning it goes *pop*.

Louise Culley (11)
St Columb Major CP School

MY DOG

My dog is very big,
He has long droopy ears,
And big sharp teeth.
He is very fluffy.
He lives in a garage.
He also has his own little sofa.

Rosina Pappin
St Columb Major CP School

SNOWSTORM

The wind crashes on the window,
Lightning strikes everywhere.
Clouds as black
As a witch's cat.
Rain tapping on the window,
Snow coming down everywhere,
But wait, it's stopped!

Christine Billingham (8)
St Columb Major CP School

DILAN

He wakes me up in the night,
And then we have a fight.
After the fight we wake my sister up,
And give her a fright.
Then we go downstairs
And bang saucepans on each other's heads.
We get bread and catapult it under the bed,
After that we have a water fight.
After the water fight
He's out of sight,
Then I go to bed crying and sobbing
Because he's gone.

Joe Slack (9)
St Columb Major CP School

SAILOR

I'd like to be a sailor,
To sail the ocean blue.
I could have been a doctor
And my name would be Sue,
But I'd still like to be a sailor
To sail the open sea,
But while I'm not a sailor
I'd just like to be me.

Annie Brown (8)
St Columb Major CP School

ONE OWL

One owl flew in the night,
His head was squished 'cause his hat was too tight.
He looked around and took off his hat,
A little bug saw and said his head was fat.

This made the owl uncomfortable
So he chased a bug and it flew into a wall.
The bug felt sick and fell to the floor,
Then a lady opened the door.

The poor bug was flat
So the owl used him as a coffee mat,
Finally the bug was back to size,
Now that bug was very wise.

Danielle Wadd (9)
St Columb Major CP School

WINTER ICE

W inter is icy,
I t is cold,
N orth wind blows the snowflakes,
T he robin stays in the barn,
E verybody stays at home,
R apidly snow is falling onto the ground.

I cy weather,
C rystal white snow,
E nd of winter.

Leigh Brooks (8)
St Columb Major CP School

SPICE

My cat called Spice,
He is very nice,
He runs around the floor,
Hitting his head on the bedroom floor.

I love my cat even more,
He has sharp claws,
He always goes outside,
I sometimes give him a ride.

I love him loads,
He likes toads,
He really is the best,
He's better than the rest.

He's the best cat in the world,
He likes hair that is curled.

Jade Barrasin (9)
St Columb Major CP School

ANIMALS

A spider span a web of silk,
Goats and cows make milk.
Birds flutter in the air,
Pigs watch, stand and stare.
Caterpillars crawling on the ground . . .
While the farmer walks his hound.
If you read this before you go to bed,
All these animals will be in your head.

Shannon Smith (9)
St Columb Major CP School

WINTER WEATHER

Rainy robin in the sky,
Swirling winter clouds.
White sparkles,
Cold in the rain, wind and wet.

Foggy mist
Around small people.
Nice and warm,
Closed doors and fires.

Tin cold,
Trees sing icy songs,
Like the snow is coming.
Yes . . . the snow is coming soon.

Laura Barrasin (8)
St Columb Major CP School

WATER EVERYWHERE

There's water on the ceiling,
And water on the wall.
There's water on the landing,
And water in the hall.
There's water in the bedroom,
And water on the stair.
Whenever Daddy takes a bath
There's water everywhere.

Danielle Platt (8)
St Columb Major CP School

MY BROTHER

My brother is always annoying me,
He goes in my room
When I'm not there.
He thinks he's the best,
But he's not.
He nicks my CDs
And lies to me,
But I love my brother.

Sarah Chapman (9)
St Columb Major CP School

IF YOU WANT TO BE GREAT!

If you want to be great,
You don't need to fight or hate.

If you're really good,
You would say 'No'.
You really would.

It's no way the worst,
You put your friend first.

If you break up with your friend,
You have to try and make amends.

If you don't do all that
You might cry,
So you really have to try!

If you do have friendship,
Never ever let it slip!

Lewis Johnson (8)
St Mary's RC Primary School, Falmouth

THE SUN

The sun, the sun,
You are really fun,
Please shine down on me.

The sun, the sun,
Come out more so
We can have fun.

The sun, the sun,
You are a fried egg
In the sky.

The sun, the sun,
Always shine over me
Mr Sun.

The sun, the sun,
You are as hot as fire.
I love you Mr Sun.

Joseph Halloran (9)
St Mary's RC Primary School, Falmouth

THE WHISTLE OF THE WIND

The wind is whistling,
It seems to be telling a story,
But only in a whistle.
It's tugging on me,
Pulling harder and harder.
The trees are dancing along with the wind,
Once again the wind has passed.

Rebecca Telling (9)
St Mary's RC Primary School, Falmouth

OUR HIDING PLACE

We've got a hiding place
In my street,
We think it's cool
To rest our feet.

It's made of leaves
And sticks,
We wish it could be made of bricks.

It's really good for hide-and-seek
And we try not to peek.

Hardly anybody knows about it,
Only me and my mate,
We draw pictures and create.

It was really funny when a cat jumped down,
It sat on the tree and the tree had a crown.

Our hiding place
Is the *best!*

Emily Jorey (8)
St Mary's RC Primary School, Falmouth

WET DAYS

What should I do while it is raining?
I sit and watch the rain tapping against the window.
What should I do?
I'm so bored.

The sun won't come and the clouds won't go,
I'm still not sure what to do.
The rain's still tapping harder,
I guess the sun won't come back after all.

I watch and listen to cars going up and down the wet road,
Thinking about what I could do if the sun was out.
I tap the rhythm of the rain on the window sill,
Please! Please go away rain!

Daniel Turner (8)
St Mary's RC Primary School, Falmouth

MY AUNTIE JEAN

My auntie Jean, my auntie Jean
She is a shoe queen.
My auntie Jean, my auntie Jean
She watches QVC and makes a gorgeous cup of tea.
My auntie Jean, my auntie Jean
She drinks at cocktail bars, she looks like a movie star.
My auntie Jean, my auntie Jean
She eats cows' udders and pigs' feet, it's a real treat.
My auntie Jean, my auntie Jean,
Her wardrobe is like a chest, it suits her the best.
My auntie Jean, my auntie Jean
She goes shopping every day, she has plenty of money to pay.
My auntie Jean, my auntie Jean
She likes to eat Spam and has a great tan.
My auntie Jean, my auntie Jean
She plants bright, pretty flowers, they grow so high like
                                            the Eiffel Tower.
My auntie Jean, my auntie Jean
She has a daughter who is crazy like cousin Daisy.
My auntie Jean, my auntie Jean
She adores the sun and likes cinnamon buns.
My auntie Jean, my auntie Jean
Every hour with her is a thrill, she is brill, brill, brill.

Daisy Roberts (9)
St Mary's RC Primary School, Falmouth

I Love Babies!

Teddies and rattles
Cause big hassles.
Big red cheeks,
The milk bottle always leaks.

Holding the baby,
The cute little thing,
He's wriggling and dribbling
All over me.

He loves his milk,
Slurp! Slurp! Slurp!
Burp! Burp! Burp!
He turns blue
Every hour or two.

I love babies,
All cute, really cute!
I love babies just as much as you.

Thomas Edgerton (8)
St Mary's RC Primary School, Falmouth

Autumn

Amber leaves fall to the ground,
Twisting and twirling all around,
Hundreds of leaves spread.
Yellowy leaves fly down on the ground,
Blowing around,
Yellow leaves remind me of beautiful, naked trees.
Golden leaves fly up into the autumn cup
But then the cup dries up.

Jake Scrace (8)
St Mary's RC Primary School, Falmouth

MY GREAT UNCLE

My great uncle,
He is absolutely excellent.
He is more than excellent,
He takes me to lots of places.

My great uncle
Is better than the rest.
He doesn't take a break.
We do some great things,
Like climbing some slippery rocks,
We have a great time.

When we get home
We are covered in muck and dirt.
We have yummy soup for tea.
We go and wash the muck off ourselves.
Fantastic supper,
Now it's time to go to bed,
Goodnight!

Senara Chesher (8)
St Mary's RC Primary School, Falmouth

THE SHINING MOON

The shining moon is a banana with icing on.
The moon is a bent spoon that got stuck on
A blue blanket with plates all around it.
The moon has got servants called stars,
With many stories hidden behind it.

Coral Andrewartha (8)
St Mary's RC Primary School, Falmouth

BIRD OF PREY

Flying high in the sky,
Oh bird of prey.
Swooping and diving, hovering and gliding,
Defeating your opponents,
Oh bird of prey.
Proud and brave, outwitting your enemies,
Putting them into a grave,
Oh bird of prey.
Your eyes as dark as alleyways at night,
And your competitor's chasing you, and your tail
Into a tremendous battle,
Oh bird of prey.
Your foes are defeated,
Oh bird of prey.

Marty Conlon (8)
St Mary's RC Primary School, Falmouth

THE MOON

The moon is a butter biscuit,
It glitters in the sky,
It's been there for a long time,
Very, very high.

The moon glistens,
The moon gleams,
The stars follow it through the forbidden night.

Cody Cooke (8)
St Mary's RC Primary School, Falmouth

AT THE SEASIDE

The wavy sea rocks,
The sandcastle drops,
Children are upset,
People getting wet,
The wavy sea rocks.

The rocks are black,
I turn my back,
I hear a bouncing ball
As it falls,
The rocks are black.

The water is calm,
There is no harm,
The people in the water,
Some people caught,
The water is calm.

The sunset's gone,
There is no one,
Today's been fun,
I've had a bun,
The sunset's gone.

The sea turns grey,
One time each day,
The shells are down
On this town,
The sea turns grey.

The moon is reflecting,
The shells are collecting,
The sand is wet
Just like my pet,
The moon is reflecting.

Sally Morrison (8)
St Mary's RC Primary School, Falmouth

PIANO

Keys like teeth about to fall out,
It has already lost a few,
I don't know why,
But when you rub them it doesn't squeak,
It just goes from high to low or low to high.

Lid like mouth opening and closing,
It is usually open, playing a tune,
If not it will be closed, sleeping,
On the mouth it squeaks instead of not making a noise,
At night it waits till morning.

Pedals like feet dancing on the spot,
They usually stay still,
Too embarrassed to dance,
Sometimes it taps to the tune,
The feet should move forever!

Samuel Richardson-May (8)
St Mary's RC Primary School, Falmouth

AUTUMN

Leaves fly to the ground,
Trees go bare all around us,
Whistling winds come by,
The trees shiver,
A bed of leaves start forming on the ground,
The tree waits for the sun to come out,
He dreams woody dreams
While animals hibernate underneath him.

Rebecca Parsons (9)
St Mary's RC Primary School, Falmouth

FIRE WOLF

Fire wolf, your belly is like a cushion, you are so bushy, warm and soft.
Fire wolf, your legs are like furry handles off a brush.
Fire wolf, your tail is like a bushy pillow.
Fire wolf, your head is like a teddy.
Fire wolf, fire wolf, fire wolf, you're so soft everywhere.
Fire wolf, your paws glow red at night and you growl like a volcano.
Fire wolf, your ears are like trumpets.
Fire wolf, your teeth are like razors.
Fire wolf, your claws are like lead out of a pencil.
Fire wolf, fire wolf, fire wolf, you are the best.

Jake Pellow (8)
St Mary's RC Primary School, Falmouth

THE DARK SHADOW

The dark shadow dry and cold,
more evil than ever told.

The dark shadow dead and gone,
never to return to life.

The dark shadow an old thief,
stole the most precious of gold.

The dark shadow lives in the cellar,
eats what he sees.

The dark shadow's slippery eyes
can see a mile off.

Paul Bacchus (8)
St Mary's RC Primary School, Falmouth

THE GHOST

The ghost at the spooky haunted house
Is as white as a sheet,
But when you meet, you'll have a fright,
Which will make your fingers go really tight.
So I'll tell you how to get there,
That's if you don't easily scare,
You go past Ghost Post Office,
Then you hear bumbling and rumbling,
Follow it, you're at the haunted house!
You'll hear music, it's coming from the haunted house,
You'll open the gate hanging from a nail,
You'll walk up the slimy path,
You'll open the door,
You'll walk up the stairs,
And there's the ghost!

Katie Dunford (8)
St Mary's RC Primary School, Falmouth

THE MOON

The moon is a banana with eyes and a hat.
The moon is a cookie, other people say,
With cream sauce dribbling over the top.
Some say it's a firework that got stuck and won't come down.
Some people imagine it is a curtain that God uses to shut out the dark.
Others, well they think it's a lantern,
When it's dark the rustling of the wind blows it out,
And I think that the moon is a big round face that cheers up at night.

Elliot Webb (8)
St Mary's RC Primary School, Falmouth

THE STARS

The stars glitter in the sky
Just like a glass crystal
In the darkness.

The stars are like a dazzling
White sparkling egg,
In the forbidden night.

The stars, the stars brighten
Up the gloomy moonless night.

The stars, the stars go away
At the gleaming sun of dawn.

Daniel Rudall (8)
St Mary's RC Primary School, Falmouth

MY VILLAGE

In St Tudy
there is an angry slide,
slithering through the
grumpy, greasy grass.

In St Tudy
there is an old, orange
oak tree, towering
over the village like
a giant giraffe.

In St Tudy
there is a cheating church,
sprinting silently
through the noisy village.

Poppy Yeomans (8)
St Tudy CE Primary School, Bodmin

IN ST TUDY

In St Tudy the flowers dance in the breeze,
It's like a river flowing in your mind,
The trees are as tall as a mountain.

In St Tudy the oak tree is like a squirrel's home,
There is a laughing sun.

In St Tudy the village is like a rocky island far away,
In St Tudy.

Jack Yeo (8)
St Tudy CE Primary School, Bodmin

WILD ST TUDY

The dark, terrible tall trees, whistling wildly
at the busy bus shelter.
The swings, swing roughly while the slide lifts
its wobbly wooden legs out of the wood-chipped ground.
The church stretches its high tower
up to the cheerful birds in the bright blue sky.
The shop rushes down the road, like a happy customer,
rushing around like a mad elephant.

Adam Matulewicz (9)
St Tudy CE Primary School, Bodmin

DARKNESS

The street lights gleaming in the moonlit street.
The swinging and swaying trees,
Stare in amazement at the rustling bushes.
The flowers sit mumbling to each other.
The roundabout spins really rapidly in the stormy wild wind.

The old oak tree stands watching
And protecting the school and ancient church.
The old swings fly around in the whistling air.
The slide as slippery as a slimy slug slithers to its home.
The street lights gleam no more.

Christopher Simmons (8)
St Tudy CE Primary School, Bodmin

A DAY IN ST TUDY

The chattering church stands
praying to God like a holy reverend.
The tall trees sit talking loudly to each other
like naughty children in a maths lesson.
The huge village hall darts about
like a cheetah catching its prey.
The old oak tree yawns slowly
like an old moaning man.
The church chatters no more.

Brian Stidwell (9)
St Tudy CE Primary School, Bodmin

A DARK NIGHT

Every night haunted houses howl to the mysterious moon.
Flowers flee frightfully from the tall great trees,
Who are dancing to a soft breeze.
The old oak tree, as old as a pair of broken scissors,
Cutting through the dusty ground, reaching for the moon.
The scary school, mysteriously stands still like a dark mist.
The church slowly slivers through the damp, greasy, green grass.
Suddenly silence falls!

Jessica Mann (7)
St Tudy CE Primary School, Bodmin

WINDY DAY

Flowers flutter in the wild wind,
While the water flows gracefully down the clink window.
The old oak tree reaches awkwardly for the sky.
The ancient, ruined bus shelter waves at all the busy
Blue busses whizzing past.
The terrifying, still school screaming its lullaby
To the dark, sleepy night.
The clink quietly yawns, extremely slowly and silently.
The slide, slithering says its prayers.

Emma Northcott (8)
St Tudy CE Primary School, Bodmin

GOD

God is a wonderful person
Who loves each and everyone.
He helps and cures sick people
And he might live near the sun.

In a church we worship Him
By praying and singing.
We pray to Him when we're at home
And inside He's listening.

God might be eating His tea right now,
He might know my future.
He might be talking to Mary
Or shouting or whispering to her.

God might be counting His angels,
Or telling them to go to bed.
God might be going Himself
With His pillow under His head.

Heidi Thomas (8)
St Wenn Primary School, Bodmin

STRANGER

On the beach it's calm and still
As people are walking by,
Someone might be watching the sun go down
In the colourful sky.

In the evenings the sky
Is a lovely pinky blue,
While you are watching the sun go down
You feel someone's watching you.

As you look behind you
There's no one there,
A shadow just went behind the rock
On your way back up the beach,
You fear something and shout, 'Please stop.'

Back at your house they've decided not to scare you,
They went out the door in a few minutes or ten.
I'm sorry I can't give you any more information,
But this is how this poem must end.

Sophie Thomas (10)
St Wenn Primary School, Bodmin

WIND

Wind can be big or small.
Wind can be rough or kind.
Wind can fly kites or sailboats.
Wind can build or destroy.
What would we be without wind?

Michael Clarke
St Wenn Primary School, Bodmin

THE LOST CROSS

I stood on a bridge on a warm summer's day,
Next to a meadow, the stream wound its way.
A flicker of silver, just caught my eye,
I paddled across to where something might lie,
Attached to a chain was a beautiful cross,
How did it get there? It must have been lost.
I called to my sister; she helped to put it on,
But the chain was all rusty and didn't last long.
I treasured the cross and put it away
In a little pink box for ten years and a day.
I happened by chance to find it one night,
The eve of my wedding, what a beautiful sight.
I borrowed a chain from my grandmother's drawer
To wear at my wedding so it could shine once more.
For thirty-three years I showed off that cross,
I often wondered just how it was lost.
I stood by the same stream one evening in May,
The buttercups golden, the grandchildren played.
The cross and the chain both fell to the water,
I cried out in vain and called to my daughter.
Although we all searched till well after tea,
I realised that cross had never belonged to me.

Min Kybett (11)
St Wenn Primary School, Bodmin

HIDDEN TREASURE

Under the sea I can see a small boat,
There is some blue fish,
A shark guarding a treasure box,
Six green, slimy seaweed.

Under the sea I can see jellyfish looking at me.
Under the sea I can see pink and purple shells.
Under the sea I can see crabs coming next to me.
Under the sea I can see anything that I want to see.

Leepa Begum (9)
Sandy Hill Primary School

LEMON SHARK

L   emon sharks have sharp teeth.
E   ating their prey.
M   en swimming with them.
O   ver the seabed they swim.
N   ets are their enemies.

S   ee them glitter in the sea.
H   unting their prey.
A   mbush is now, as they catch dinner.
R   ipping up food.
K   illing big fish.

Sam Woolhouse (10)
Sandy Hill Primary School

HIDDEN TREASURES

T   he first baby tooth I had.
R   ubber that I kept for ever.
E   lephant clock I had two years ago.
A   pples with pips inside.
S   lide I had two years ago.
U   nder my bed I found my favourite pen.
R   ed ted my favourite teddy.
E   ggs with chicks inside.

Kelly Maby (9)
Sandy Hill Primary School

HIDDEN TREASURES

H idden treasures are very valuable.
I can see lemon and great white sharks all around us.
D eeper and deeper we go in the sea.
D ivers hope to find lots of treasure.
E very day you see divers going in the deep blue sea.
N ever go near the great white sharks.

T alented divers love to explore.
R apid waves distracted the divers.
E meralds are very rare.
A t night lots of dangerous sea creatures come out.
S ilver and gold necklaces, ring and bracelets can be found.
U nder the sea I can see lots of fish, but no hidden treasure.
R usty ships with hidden treasures in them.
E gyptian seas have lots of hidden treasures in them.
S unset is a great time to look for hidden treasures.

Hannah Goodwin (9)
Sandy Hill Primary School

TREASURE

T reasure looking like little insects in the pool.
R eally interesting tadpoles.
E lephants running all over the treasure.
A nts crawling up and down the trees.
S ea crashing against the rocks.
U nder the umbrella trying to keep you dry.
R oaring lions looking for their prey.
E normous monkeys swinging tree to tree.

   Treasure is fun!

Kimberley Johns (10)
Sandy Hill Primary School

MY MARBLE

In a marble
I can see mothers
Shouting at their children.
I can see bright fire
Coming from a dragon's breath.
I can see children
Playing in the playground.
I can see giants
Destroying people's lovely homes.
I can see children
Fooling round in the classroom.
I can see greedy robbers
Stealing from a bank.
I can see cars
Driving on the old dusty road.
If I wasn't there I wouldn't be
As happy as can be.
That's my marble.

Matthew Pope (10)
Sandy Hill Primary School

HIDDEN TREASURES

My hidden treasures are deep in the jungle
With fierce lions, tigers guarding the gate,
Leeches guarding the floor in a bundle,
They wait for people and eat them all up,
No one's allowed past the gate,
There's a special treasure inside,
Emeralds, diamonds, rubies, gold,
Are you taking the risk?

Kimberley Mills (10)
Sandy Hill Primary School

HIDDEN TREASURES

My hidden treasures are under the beautiful sea,
Mediterranean, Atlantic, where could it be?
A gold palace, sapphires, diamonds,
New species of dolphins and eels called eyemonds.
Mer people shield the underwater treasures
For the Atlantic King has the key and often measures.
Golden walls and chambers filled with silver too,
Bronze pearls that didn't look old but new.
The treasures were diamonds and crystals
But the King's powers were like sharpened thistles.
The only way to get the treasures was to get the key,
The mer people will be free, and will be the same to me.
My treasures are under the sea,
Where you could be for ever.

Charmaine Vague (10)
Sandy Hill Primary School

HIDDEN TREASURE

My nan had a necklace,
A beautiful, gold necklace
Until one day she gave it to me.
It must be treasure I thought, it must be.
So I asked my mum,
I asked my dad
If it was treasure, they said no,
But I believe with all my heart
That it is treasure, hidden treasure.

Kate David (9)
Sandy Hill Primary School

HIDDEN TREASURES

A little green marble that holds all the sky,
Four porcelain dolls simply dressed,
Richly dressed with beautiful long, long hair,
A simple slate necklace I wear every day,
A tiny baby in my mother's tummy,
All of them hidden, hidden away in dolls' prams
In boxes, in pockets, in people,
All these you might not think are special
But they are very special to me,
Very special indeed.

Philippa Anderson (9)
Sandy Hill Primary School

HIDDEN TREASURE

My grandmother's watch,
Silver and old.
A gold ring
I found in the sea.
My first baby tooth,
My best toy,
Old with holes.
My grandfather's old suitcase,
Inside is an army suit,
Mouldy and dusty,
His diary tattered and torn.
What treasures I have.

Kaylee Harrison (10)
Sandy Hill Primary School

HIDDEN TREASURES

H is treasure box has fifty pounds in it.
I have a Ferrari sign.
D o you have some treasures?
D own under my bed,
E xciting treasures for me,
N ew treasures.

T he fossils hidden in the mud.
R ain is for the desert.
E ggs for Easter,
A s everybody opens their presents.
S and hides lots of things.
U nder Tim's bed there's a skateboard.
R emember your hidden treasures,
E ach one
S pecial.

James Palmer (9)
Sandy Hill Primary School

IN THE FIRE I CAN SEE...

I can see red and orange flames.
I can see dragons breathing fire.
I can see steamy bluebells.
I can see marbles rolling around.
I can see children running and laughing.
I can see teachers shouting and raising their fists.
I can see flowers glittering in the sun.
I can see flames sparkling.
I can see fierce snakes slithering around.

Laura Shepperd (10)
Sandy Hill Primary School

HIDDEN TREASURES

H idden in my room
I have a ring I dug up from the ground,
D irty and rusty,
D im and dull,
E very day I look at it,
N o one will take it away from me.

T he ring is a power of some sort.
R ings are silver and gold.
E veryone knows about it.
A lways shiny and beautiful.
S ilver and gold,
U nder the ground waiting to be found.
R ings are really different,
E yes gleam when they see it.
S ecret in my box.

Matt Trethewey (10)
Sandy Hill Primary School

HIDDEN TREASURE

T he camera I got for Christmas.
R uption skateboard.
E ngland the country I live in.
A nd the big hi-fi,
S urround sound as well.
U nofficial magazines.
R ed Arrows a special treat,
E xciting to look at,
S o, so precious.

Paul Gill (10)
Sandy Hill Primary School

HIDDEN TREASURES

My favourite treasures are
My PlayStation games,
My computer games,
My army men,
My telly,
My board games,
My friendly games,
My little den
And my bowl of jelly.

My treasures that are hidden are
Pieces of gold under the sea,
They will glisten at you and me.
An old game found in a loft,
I'll have a go but it will be tough.
An old box found on the mountains,
I'll look inside,
I'll wonder what's inside,
It'll probably be nothing.

Barney Mathews (9)
Sandy Hill Primary School

HIDDEN TREASURE

Under the sea I saw a man, but it wasn't real, it was made of gold.
Under the sea I saw different coloured fish.
Under the sea I saw loads of seaweed, different coloured seaweed.
Under the sea I saw a treasure box full of gold and silver.
Under the sea I saw a shark, but luckily it wasn't real,
It was made of silver.
Under the sea I saw a basking shark, I thought it was fake
But it wasn't and then he ate me.

Ryan Boxall (9)
Sandy Hill Primary School

I WENT TO THE FUTURE

I went to the future
For a day or two,
I didn't stay long
It was so sad and blue.
The people lived in shiny domes,
Smoke filled the air,
I really can't imagine who would like to live there.
Nobody ever went there,
The land was grey, cold and bare
Except for rubbish here and there.
There were no plants, not any more,
Except for one shoot, ragged and poor,
I sat there kneeling by its side as it wilted,
And slowly died.
So next time you put
Rubbish in the bin,
Recycle it and save this world you're in.

Emily Hinkley (10)
Shortlanesend Primary School

MY CAT

My cat was black,
Not a fighter jet type of cat,
He has never bitten or scratched,
His miaow was very friendly,
Greeting people with it.
Furry, cuddly,
His name was Sooty,
But now he's passed away.

Brandon Light (9)
Shortlanesend Primary School

MY PERSIAN KITTEN CALLED PILLOW

My beautiful Persian kitten called Pillow
Arches her back, with such an elegant air,
She really seems like royalty,
I watch as she stretches her delicate legs,
And I see her pad into the kitchen.

She's learnt how to open the fridge door,
And she picks up her own special milk carton,
And carries it in her mouth to her bowl,
So I pour some in for her.

She puts out her glossy pink tongue,
And laps some of it up,
Then mews at her empty food bowl
I give her some cat food which she sniffs
Suspiciously, and then starts eating.

When she's finished her meal,
She pads back to her rug in front of the fire,
And settles down for a snooze.
I really love my Persian kitten called Pillow.

Suzanne Reeves (10)
Shortlanesend Primary School

THE GINGER CAT

The ginger cat is waking up,
Her eyes blue as the sky,
She stands on all fours,
And shows her claws and yawns.

Then she goes for something to eat,
With her lip bent down slightly.
Then she arches her back as far as it goes
And lets herself down on her delicate toes,
And goes for a drink of milk.

She opens her mouth
And out comes her tongue,
Then licks it all up
Until it's gone,
And pads away with her tail high in the air.

Rachel Parry (9)
Shortlanesend Primary School

SARA'S NUMEROUS SNAKES

My name's Sara, I had snakes
Until they died!
First Colin the cobra
Who came from Dover,
He was a very naughty little snake
Because he hit me with a rake
And now he's a real moaner.
Then there was Alan, the adder
Who climbed up a ladder,
He was ever so high,
Decided to fly
And now he's much sadder.
Third was Paul the python
Who couldn't pronounce a hyphen,
He was dead pretty soon
Because he ate my favourite balloon,
Now he's aboard the Lybython.
Last of all there was Roland the rattlesnake
Who ate my sister's birthday cake,
And as well as that
He ate my cat,
So now he's in Windsor lake.
I think I'll stick to hamsters!

Hayley Robins (11)
Shortlanesend Primary School

TWINKLE, TWINKLE CHOCOLATE BAR

Twinkle, twinkle chocolate bar,
I'm feeling hungry I'll buy you from the Spar.
I'll gobble you up and scream you will
Unless you give me dinner and pay my bill!

Holly Wenna-Hegarty (10)
Shortlanesend Primary School

UNTITLED

A stupid dog,
A lazy dog,
A very annoying dog,
A fat dog,
A sloppy dog,
A howling dog,
A boy dog,
A girl dog,
What next?

Annette Hodges (10)
Shortlanesend Primary School

LITTLE BOY SAM

A little boy, Sam
Was eating some ham,
And sat on a toadstool one day
He put down some hay to keep spiders away,
But the spiders were busy eating jam!

Adam Wells (10)
Shortlanesend Primary School

THE GHOSTS AT SCHOOL

At our school we've got ghosts,
The ghoul that haunts the store cupboard,
The ghost that lives in the boys' toilets,
The poltergeist that lives in the staffroom,
The spectre that lives in the PE shed,
The spirit that loves football,
The gloomy nun who eats all the food,
The ghostly dog that eats homework,
And the phantom that eats children and teachers.

Gareth Reeves (10)
Shortlanesend Primary School

THE PEST OF 2002

The pest of 2002
Weed in my shoe!

The swift hopper
Was the carrot dropper!

The slight nibbler
Was a furry listener!

A hole digger
And a cute little squeaker!

Aimee Wonnacott (10)
Shortlanesend Primary School

I AM

I am the wind, blowing around.
I am the snow, lay down on the ground.
I am the sun, blazing bright.
I am the hail, as a thundering fright.

I am a star, up in the sky.
I am a bird, flying so high.
I am the yellow, dusty sand.
I am the wrinkle, on someone's hand.

I am a spider's web, made from silk.
I am a baby's bottle, filled with milk.
I am a drip, from melting ice.
I am a gang of squeaking mice.

I am a note, from wandering sound.
I am some glitter, spread all around.
I am a clump, of gathering trees,
Swirling and whirling, with the breath of the breeze.

What are you?

Rosalind Lytham (8)
Tregony CP School

SHAMPOO

Shampoo in the shower every hour,
Slish, slosh have a wash,
It will do you no harm,
Wash your face in every place,
And on your arm,
So slish, slosh, do please have a wash!

Rowan Heather (10)
Tregony CP School

MY PET HAMSTER

My pet hamster is a bit of a pain,
He drives you up the wall and makes you go insane.
He loves his little wheel going round and round,
It makes your head go pound, pound, pound.
He doesn't like the light
So he tries to get out with all his might.
He has a big cage with lots of tubes
And when he eats his cheeks go like balloons.
In the night you cannot sleep
Because you can hear him in his wheel with his tapping little feet,
And by the way his name is Rampster,
My pet hamster.

Verity McIntosh (10)
Tregony CP School

WEATHER

Rain, rain you are a pain,
Just go away,
Let the sun come and play.
I wonder,
Why there's thunder.
When there's a flash of lightning,
It is frightening.
I like to go sailing
When it's raining.
I hope the sun comes out to play today.

Daniel Grayston (9)
Tregony CP School

I'M TELLING ON YOU!

I'm telling on you,
You put egg on my nose,
It dripped and ruined my clothes!
I'm telling on you,
You put cheese on my face
And ham on my pencil case!
I'm telling on you,
You put cake on my chin,
Then slammed it in the bin!
I'm telling on you,
You ate my last eclair
And squirted sauce in my hair!
I'm scare of you,
You're bigger than me,
You're stronger than me!
I'm hiding from you,
But when I get out
I'm telling on you!

Daisy Elizabeth Jones (11)
Tregony CP School

MY WISH

Everyone has got a dog except for me
I wish I had a Labrador,
They try to run after cats, but they can't win.
I wish I had a Labrador,
They're good at exercise,
I wish I had a Labrador,
Trust me I'll train it well, and give it all my love,
I wish I had a Labrador.

Daniel Campbell-Harris (10)
Upton Cross Primary School

EYES ON STICKS

They came down to Earth, that's when I knew they existed,
Their eyes were on sticks,
They spoke a foreign language,
I think they said hello,
Then they sang a song,
The words were,
'Zip zap zoo noo noo noo ding dang dong do do do'.
All of a sudden they shouted, 'Oo la la!'
I think they meant go away!
But I just stood and stopped and said,
'No! I've lost my baby ted.'
I scared them all by telling them he'll eat you.
They pulled their fazors from their pockets,
Then shot off up in their rockets.
No I think you know their alien type,
Well give yourselves a tick,
Cos you are right!

Emily-Rose Clay (10)
Upton Cross Primary School

BUTTERFLY

Butterfly, butterfly where do you fly?
High and low
All over the sky.
Fluttering there, fluttering here,
Fluttering everywhere.
Wings like church windows,
Brilliant and bright;
The colours of the rainbow,
What a beautiful sight.

Millie Parrott (8)
Upton Cross Primary School

THE ZOO OF DOOM!

A is for Antony who eats all the ants.
B is for Bertrick who loses his pants.
C is for Christine who always gets stuck.
D is for Daniel who has a bath in the muck.
E is for Ellie who loves to pick flowers.
F is for Frederick who always breaks showers.
G is for Gary who works in a garage.
H is for Hannah who loves to get married.
I is for Ian who eats all the pies.
J is for Jasmine who wants to die.
K is for Katy who loves to go out.
L is for Lucia who is the loudest to *shout!*
M is for Mum who loves me too much.
N is for Norma who wears a green jumper.
O is for Oliver who lives on a boat.
P is for Polly who makes a little moat.
Q is for Queen who acts rather posh.
R is for Roger who makes a great fuss.
S is for Sian who loves to ring doorbells.
T is for Tommy who always really smells.

    This is the end of my poem,
    I hope it made you laugh.
    This is the end of my poem,
    Now I am going for a bath.

Danielle Elizabeth Mayors (9)
Upton Cross Primary School

BEE

I buzz, buzz and buzz
Because I am a bee,
I never rest
In my own nest,
I buzz around with glee.

I filled up my beehive
From loads of flowers,
It took five hours.
I love flowers,
I love building hives.

Joshua Turner (8)
Upton Cross Primary School

WHY CAN'T THEY GO TO BED?

I've got butterflies in my tummy,
Elephants in my head,
Giraffes at my feet,
Why can't they go to bed?

I've got monkeys on the windows,
Hanging upside down,
I've got tigers who just sit all night
And give a ferocious frown.

I've got parrots who just chatter,
They get on my nerves,
So I lock them up inside their cage
Cos that's what they deserve.

I really want to read this book,
So please just go away,
I'll welcome you with open arms
If you come another day.

All these noises while I'm reading
They really do annoy,
But underneath I really know they're
Only just my toys.

Kathy Dilworth (10)
Upton Cross Primary School

How Many Clouds?

How many clouds are there?
More than ten.
More than I can count.

How many clouds are there?
More than a hundred.
More than we can count.

How many clouds are there?
More than history.
More than anyone can count.

Whispy, white, angry, dull,
More than more.
How many are there?
Tell me.

Gemma Stephens (10)
Upton Cross Primary School

Love

Love is the warmth of the fire,
the heart of a human being.

Love is happiness for you and me,
it hangs over the rainbow like a star.

Love is the flutter of a butterfly,
the petals of a flower.

Love is easy to break
so hold it gently in your hand.

Carys Barriball (8)
Upton Cross Primary School

SUNSET

Over the hill I see the unicorn standing by the sunset,
Down by the lake I see a glance of the rainbowfish
Jumping in the water,
Swooping by the mountains I look for the eagle catching its prey.

Sitting on the treetop I see a swish of the monkey
Playing with his friends,
Laying in the house I peer at the cat sleeping on the small mat,
Over the hill I see the unicorn standing by the sunset.

Standing in the distance I spot the owl hooting on the tree,
Playing by the stream I saw the lion growling in the water,
Over the hill I see the unicorn standing by the sunset.

Flying over the river I gaze upon the butterfly fluttering in the sky,
Soaring through the forest I squint to see the buzzard's tail
In the moonlight,
Over the hill I see the unicorn standing by the sunset.

Gliding over the moor I stare at the magpie catching worms,
Jumping through the valley I peer at the deer,
Over the hill I see the unicorn standing by the sunset.

Lucia Szweda (9)
Upton Cross Primary School

A CAT IN A BIN

A cat in a bin
Got covered in banana skin.
He smelt like apple peel,
So he let out an enormous squeal.

Terry Northey (8)
Upton Cross Primary School

The Sun The Moon

The sun

The sun round and juicy,
Making people brown,
People in the sea swimming upside down,
My friend on a dolphin,
Me on a whale,
We were both swimming free,
With a swish of his tail.

The moon

The moon in a banana shape,
The shadows that it makes,
Makes the water glisten,
And lights up the night.

Victoria Anne Moyse (9)
Upton Cross Primary School

My Broom Was Magic

I fly, I fly so high,
It's so much fun to be so high.
When I'm in bed I wait till
My mum and dad are in bed,
I fly, I fly so high in the sky.
It is so much fun
To be so high in the dark gloomy sky,
I see the green grass down below,
I pass the long windy roads,
Now it's time to go home,
I did have lots of fun tonight!

Mark Weeks (8)
Upton Cross Primary School

WHEN I WENT ON MY TRAVELS

When I went on my travels
To see the Queen,
I met a lot of queer people,
Have you seen,
The witch that sits on the mat
With her big fat cat,
The mayor that sits on the pot
And the boy that miaows a lot?

When I went on my travels
To see the Queen,
I met a lot of strange creatures.
Have you seen,
The hippo with a horn
And a tiger that's bored,
A bear that's blue,
A pig that's pink and flies over the loo?

When I went on my travels
To see the Queen,
I saw a lot of weird views.
Have you seen,
The mountain called Ziggy,
A house looking like a zoo,
The statue of a pig
That says, 'Toodle Oo'?

Well I've been on my travels
And I've seen the Queen.
There are a lot of strange creatures that I haven't seen
Like a dog and a cat and a mouse
And a bunny rabbit that's been left loose in the house.

Georgina Lucas (10)
Upton Cross Primary School

TEDDY BEAR

My teddy bear is like a friend
Sometimes I think he's real and
Nothing in the world (I think)
Will change the way I feel
He's silent when I need him
He's silent when I'm sad
And sometimes when I think
Or know that I've been very bad
He doesn't blame, he doesn't shout
He doesn't curse or swear
He sits over there without any cares
My teddy bear is like a friend
Sometimes I think he's real
And nothing in the world (I think)
Will change the way I feel.

Elizabeth Joy Cowan (10)
Upton Cross Primary School

UNDER MY BED

When I go to see my uncle Fred
He tells me stories about under my bed.
So when I go to bed at night
I think about it, it gives me such a fright.
My mummy doesn't really care,
She really should believe me, it's so not fair.
So now before I go to sleep
I take a quick look under my white bed sheet.
But one night I looked under my bed,
I took a peep and *boo!* It was uncle Fred.

Holly Beale (9)
Upton Cross Primary School

THE ANGELS

The angels I saw up there fly
I know they looked at me.
For the angels I saw up there fly
Were looking down on me.

They know what heavens look like
And how pretty they can be.

They saw how mankind made his world,
And how each thing was placed on Earth,
And shed a tear for the Earth.
The angels I saw up there fly were looking down on me.

Catherine Cole (9)
Upton Cross Primary School

THE WEIRDEST PLACES

Fish in the family room
Lion in the lounge
Cat in the kitchen
Hamster in the hall
Bat in the bathroom
Duck in the den
Dolphin in the dining room
Snake in the study
Tortoise in the toilet
Ant in the attic
Rats in the roof
Goats in the garage
Animals get in the weirdest places.

Katy Bartlett (10)
Upton Cross Primary School

MY UNCLE FRED

My uncle Fred,
He just stays in bed,
The lazy so-and-so,
And he only plays in snow.

My uncle Fred,
He told Ted,
He would get wed,
In his bed.

My uncle Fred,
He always said,
That I should always know,
When to come and go.

Louise Grace Barriball (10)
Upton Cross Primary School

DOGS, DOGS

Dogs, dogs
Dalmatian dogs
In the dairy
And in the fog.

Dogs, dogs
Different colours
They like playing with your
Sisters and brothers.

Dogs, dogs
Chew up their toys
Scatters at their families
Especially boys.

Emma Bunney (9)
Upton Cross Primary School

My Three Pets

My cat she is a stupid cat,
She's very plump and short,
For when the mice come out to play,
She brings in what she's caught.

My rabbit who does bounce around,
He doesn't stop and stare,
For when we go to pick him up,
It ends up as a dare.

My mouse is quite a sick mouse,
He does not like to squeak,
He has to dodge around a bit,
To avoid the trampling feet.

My three pets they're not alike,
They're not at all the same,
They scramble round and make a noise,
They make it seem a game.

Alice Colligan (10)
Upton Cross Primary School

Untitled

My gran has an eye in the back of her head
She can see me when I sneak out of bed.
When I creep downstairs to have a snack
She catches me and gives me a smack.

But my mum has x-ray vision
She can see what I watch on television.
When I say I've tidied my room
She knows I haven't and gives out a boom.

Adam Carthew (10)
Upton Cross Primary School

THE THING IN THE SHED!

On Monday I did lose,
My knickers and my shoes,
I looked for mine,
But had no time,
So went to school *quite* nude.

On Tuesday my legs did show,
I looked up high and low,
My jeans have gone,
To where and beyond,
Now I'm bare below.

On Wednesday I made up my mind,
These things I was going to find,
I went out the door,
Then heard a great roar,
And ended up back inside.

On Thursday I woke from my snooze,
And collected the morning news,
I looked for my top,
Found it I did not,
Now nothing is left to lose.

On Friday I opened the door,
Nothing was left but the floor,
I stared round the house,
Not even a mouse,
Survived from this great roar.

Let this teach you I implore,
That if you hear a roar,
Grab your socks and knickers,
And hide them in your drawer!

Bethany Louise Plummer (11)
Upton Cross Primary School